# Soviet Economic Planning, 1965–1980

# Westview Replica Editions

The concept of Westview Replica Editions is a response to the continuing crisis in academic and informational publishing. Library budgets for books have been severely curtailed. Ever larger portions of general library budgets are being diverted from the purchase of books and used for data banks, computers, micromedia, and other methods of information retrieval. Interlibrary loan structures further reduce the edition sizes required to satisfy the needs of the scholarly community. Economic pressures (particularly inflation and high interest rates) on the university presses and the few private scholarly publishing companies have severely limited the capacity of the industry to properly serve the academic and research communities. As a result, many manuscripts dealing with important subjects, often representing the highest level of scholarship, are no longer economically viable publishing projects—or, if accepted for publication, are typically subject to lead times ranging from one to three years.

Westview Replica Editions are our practical solution to the problem. We accept a manuscript in camera-ready form, typed according to our specifications, and move it immediately into the production process. As always, the selection criteria include the importance of the subject, the work's contribution to scholarship, and its insight, originality of thought, and excellence of exposition. The responsibility for editing and proofreading lies with the author or sponsoring institution. We prepare chapter headings and display pages, file for copyright, and obtain Library of Congress Cataloging in Publication Data. A detailed manual contains simple instructions for preparing the final typescript, and our editorial staff is always available to answer questions.

The end result is a book printed on acid-free paper and bound in sturdy library-quality soft covers. We manufacture these books ourselves using equipment that does not require a lengthy make-ready process and that allows us to publish first editions of 300 to 600 copies and to reprint even smaller quantities as needed. Thus, we can produce Replica Editions quickly and can keep even very specialized books in print as long as there is a demand for them.

# About the Book and Author

## Soviet Economic Planning, 1965-1980
### Fyodor I. Kushnirsky

In studying Soviet economic planning, Western analysts frequently are guided by official Soviet literature and legislative acts, which reflect only the facade of the economic structure and reveal little about actual planning practice. The author of this book draws on 14 years of experience as a planning researcher in the Soviet Union to provide a first-hand analysis of how Soviet economic planning actually works.

Dr. Kushnirsky explores the two fundamental changes in the Soviet economy that have gained prominence in the Brezhnev era: centralization in decision making, and the strong role of party institutions in economic activity (eliminated by Khrushchev, but flourishing again under Brezhnev). Although it is widely believed that the 1965 Economic Reform was a move toward decentralization, Dr. Kushnirsky shows that its primary effect was the centralization of economic management, with the long-term result of economic deterioration in the republics and provincial regions. Providing a framework for understanding future developments in the Soviet economy, this book also assesses the relationship of the planner to the basic economic system and describes the principles, organizational structure, and methodology of planning in the Soviet Union.

From 1965 to 1978, Fyodor I. Kushnirsky headed a team of researchers at the Ukrainian branch of the Scientific Research Institute for Planning and Norms in the Soviet Union. He is the author of several books and many articles on economic planning and currently is visiting associate professor of Economics at Temple University, where he is conducting research on econometric modeling of the Soviet economy.

# Soviet Economic Planning, 1965–1980

## Fyodor I. Kushnirsky

Westview Press / Boulder, Colorado

*A Westview Replica Edition*

Copyright © 1982 by Westview Press, Inc.

Published in 1982 in the United States of America by
     Westview Press, Inc.
     5500 Central Avenue
     Boulder, Colorado 80301
     Frederick A. Praeger, President and Publisher

Library of Congress Cataloging in Publication Data
Kushnirsky, Fyodor I.
     Soviet economic planning, 1965-1980.
     (A Westview replica edition)
     Bibliography: p.
     Includes index.
     1. Soviet Union--Economic policy--1966-1970.  2. Soviet Union--Economic
policy--1971-1975.  3. Soviet Union--Economic policy--1976-1980.  I. Title.
HC336.23.K84  1982        338.947        82-11028
ISBN 0-86531-928-6 (pbk.)


Printed and bound in the United States of America

10  9  8  7  6  5  4  3

To the memory of my father

# Contents

# Foreword

Since the early 1970s, there has been a substantial flow of Soviet emigres into the United States. This flow has included a fair number with experience as professional economists in the Soviet Union and some with experience in planning and managing the Soviet economy (although to my knowledge very few who were high placed in the planning hierarchy). These Soviet emigres have enriched our understanding of the Soviet economy. They have lectured and given courses at universities. They have participated in professional conferences. They have published articles. But, with some notable exceptions, they have rarely published specialized monographs on the workings of the Soviet economy.* To help correct this situation, Delphic Associates under the leadership of Gerold Guensberg and Robert Crowley has undertaken a program of support for the writing of technical monographs by recent Soviet emigres in a broad spectrum of the natural and social sciences. The present volume is the first, in this program, on economics.

Fyodor Kushnirsky, as he indicates in his introduction to the monograph, was until 1979 the head of a group within the Ukrainian branch of a Gosplan research

*For one such exception see Katsenelinboigen 1978 [17].

institute.  His specialty was econometrics and his
group produced the first published macroeconometric
model in the Soviet Union [10].  The present book draws
heavily on his unique background.  The work he was
engaged in for Gosplan focused on the improvement of
planning and management methods.  This involved him in
the close scrutiny and analysis of Soviet planning and
management techniques and proposals for their improvement, and in internal discussions of these matters with
people at various levels of the planning and management
bureaucracy, including some at fairly high levels of
Gosplan in Moscow.

The fact that Kushnirsky was an econometrician has
helped in making the transition from the world of
Soviet economic analysis to that of Western economic
analysis -- a transition which often proves difficult
for Soviet emigre economists.  The advantage of being
an econometrician lies in the clearly Western origins
and bases of econometrics and the relatively recent
beginnings of econometric analysis in the Soviet Union.
This has led to the establishment of methods and standards in Soviet econometrics much closer to those in
the West than is true of other fields in economics.  He
has been further aided in this transition by his
teaching and research experience in the United States.
He has been a member of the faculty of the Economics
Department at Temple University which has given him the
opportunity to interact with faculty and students.  And
he has been the principal investigator on a research
project on the regional econometric modeling of the
Soviet economy, in association with the Wharton
Centrally Planned Economies group, sponsored by the
National Council for Soviet and East European Research.
Through these teaching and research contacts he has
been helped in acquiring the analytical approach common
to economic science in the United States.  This has

added to the usefulness of his book.

Its usefulness is also enhanced by Kushnirsky's attitude toward his work. He is first and foremost a scholar. His monograph is not a diatribe of an angry emigre against the Soviet economy. He does not use it to argue the total ineptitude of Soviet planners and of the Soviet planning system. Whatever his own emotional feelings may be, he approaches his subject with a high degree of scientific objectivity. Furthermore, though he draws on his years of experience in the Soviet Union, this book is not a loose collection of personal impressions of the Soviet economy. It is a work of economic analysis, which, in addition to personal experience, draws on his research and on the research of others published in the scientific literature. And it is the mark of his scholarship that he has continued to follow the Soviet economic literature closely, as is indicated by the number of post-1979 citations of Soviet journal articles in the monograph.

The focus of Kushnirsky's study is on Soviet planning and management, primarily Gosplan and its interaction with the ministries and republican planning institutions. After an introductory chapter, the succeeding three chapters discuss: the course of management reforms after 1965; the organizational structure of Soviet planning, issues of centralization and decentralization; the methodology of Soviet planning, traditional and mathematical techniques, and attempts to computerize planning. The volume ends with some speculations about future reforms. It should be noted that this book is not an introductory text. Some knowledge of the Soviet economy on the part of the reader is required to gain full benefit from it.

What do we learn from Kushnirsky's study? There are two sources of new insights and knowledge. One is Kushnirsky's experience as an insider working in a

Gosplan institute, and the second is Kushnirsky's analysis of Soviet planning and management.

From his insider's experience as described at
various points in the monograph we gain some new information and a clearer picture of the technical operation
of Gosplan. Particularly illuminating is his section
on the distribution of functions in the planning process in which he describes the steps involved in the
construction of the five-year and annual plans and the
roles of the various departments of Gosplan and also of
the Central Committee of the Communist Party. He
informs us that each year a special internal order is
issued in Gosplan (and in the republic gosplans) which
regulates the sequence and chronology of plan construction, the interaction of all Gosplan departments and
the information each is to send and receive. At
another point, Kushnirsky describes a system of
classified internal memos signed by Gosplan department
heads in which they, at some personal risk, reveal conditions in given branches and regions of the economy as
they actually are. On the whole, his assessment of the
quality of Soviet planners is high, but this is not so
of many planning techniques. He refers to the
increased use of computers in planning as one of the
major developments since the loss of faith in the 1965
Reform. Yet his account of his own experience with the
"automated system of planning calculations" (ASPR) is
decidedly negative. He describes the contraints on
open discussion of economic issues and makes the strong
statement: "the role of economic science in economic
planning and decision making has been insignificant"
(p. 131). This is an interesting echo of the famous
statement in Stalin's Economic Problems of Socialism
that economic planning is not the job of economists,
but of policy makers.

Of particular interest, to my mind, is Kushnirsky's

illuminating description of the construction of production plans and investment plans. The dominance of the supply orientation of Soviet planning stands out clearly. Throughout his discussion, it is production capacity that determines output levels rather than reference to demand, utility, or planners' preferences. One might then assume that demand factors are reflected in investment planning. But even here the tone of Kushnirsky's discussion is on the supply side. The capacities of the capital goods producers play a major role in investment decision making.

We also learn much from Kushnirsky's own analysis of the planning phenomena that he has observed and the scientific research that he has conducted. Prominent in this group, I would include the following.

In regard to the use of economic indicators to evaluate the performance of an enterprise, Kushnirsky argues that no indicator is complete or perfect. When shortcomings appear, a new indicator is substituted for the old. Planners are constantly searching for ways of improving the system, but since they cannot propose changes in basic economic principles, they end up substituting one indicator for another, believing that the shortcomings of the former are fewer than those of the latter. 'There is always room for hope.'

To Kushnirsky, the key basic principle which prevents effective economic reform is the absence of managerial responsibility for the materials and equipment the enterprise uses. By the term managerial responsibility he means the payment for inputs out of the pockets of enterprise managers or ministers, in a sense the equivalent of enterprise owners. The absence of such managerial responsibility and thus the absence of fear of loss and bankruptcy removes a crucial constraint and determinant of effective and responsible decision making. It leads Kushnirsky to defend, for

example, the centralized material supply system in
Soviet industry. Its removal, he argues, would lead to
wholesale stealing, which would be more detrimental to
the economy than its retention.

Kushnirsky's extensive treatment of the July 1979
resolution on planning improvement is quite infor-
mative, especially his analysis of the relation between
the annual and five-year plans. His discussion of the
role of input-output methods in Soviet planning, in
which he argues that input-output cannot take the place
of material balances, is interesting, as is his advo-
cacy of the advantages of the regional administrative
system over those of the branch system. Finally, his
argument, that in recent years Gosplan has become more
attached to the Party Central Committee and its economic departments, than to the Governmental Council of
Ministers, warrants attention.

Kushnirsky's study is a valuable addition to our
literature on the Soviet economy. It is to be hoped
that it will be followed by other monographs of
knowledgeable and experienced Soviet emigres.

*Herbert S. Levine*
*Philadelphia*

# 1
# Introduction

I have been in the United States since 1979. For almost 14 years before emigrating from the Soviet Union, I was employed at the Ukrainian Branch of the Scientific Research Institute for Planning and Norms of the USSR (Ukrainskii filial Nauchno-issledovatel'skogo instituta planirovaniia i normativov pri Gosplane SSSR). I headed a team of researchers who worked in econometric modeling and forecasting of national and regional economies.

Beginning in 1969, the team created a series of econometric models for the development of the national and republic economies from the macrolevel to specific industries. The goals of this work included forecasting principal planning indicators for the 1971-1975 and 1976-1980 five-year plans and the 1976-1990 long-term plan. Among models of different levels of aggregation, the one that proved the most practical included the main macroindicators such as national income, employment, capital stock, investment, etc., and indicators for the development of various sectors of the economy (industry, agriculture and forestry, construction, transportation and communications, trade and distribution, and services) [10].

Although the Gosplan (State Planning Committee) authorities have never included the results of any

1

modeling or other research directly in plans, they can take them into consideration in preparing plan targets. In any event, the process of submitting modeling results to the authorities is always crucial and even potentially dangerous for researchers, who may lose their jobs if for some reason Gosplan rejects the results. In the cases of this which come to mind, the quality of research was in fact very low.

Despite the Institute's subordination to Gosplan USSR, its location in a republic meant that part of its research was performed for various republic planning committees. Thus my team developed econometric models not only for the country as a whole and for the Ukraine, but for Belorussia, Latvia, and Georgia as well. The information used was supplied by local planners or researchers, and the process of modeling and analysis was conducted in coordination with them.

In general, Institute research has been concentrated in the fields of methodological improvements in planning, introduction of new methods of economic stimulation, application of the normative approach to resource allocation, and computerization of planning calculations. While topics for research must be requested by the Gosplan departments, the initiative may belong to the Institute. A research plan is approved annually by the chairman of Gosplan. Does Gosplan make use of this research? We will try to answer this question and others in the general context of the present study.

The subject of the study is the activity of Gosplan USSR and its interaction with the ministries, departments, and republic planning institutions. Enterprises and the middle level of management (industry and industrial associations) will be considered only in the degree necessary to illustrate planning decisions and their implementation. The discussion of the evolution of the planning system will be based on such sources as main resolutions on planning, debates in Soviet economic literature, Soviet official statistics, and my own description and interpretation of Gosplan's performance.

The last point requires clarification. In all cases when an opinion is expressed, a reference to the source will be made. Otherwise discussions reflect the author's opinion. Some of the assertions made may be rather evident to a person familiar with the planning system, and others may be less evident. But no claim is made that these are the only truths. Everything depends on one's perceptions.

We must distinguish of course between a planning system and a planned system, which in Western terminology means a Soviet-type economy in general. The meaning of the term "planning system" that we will use is more narrow. Its organizational structure comprises all the institutions which participate in the development of national economic plans.

My evaluations of the planning system have not changed essentially since my arrival in this country. Having worked with many planners in the Soviet Union, I consider most of them well qualified for their jobs, and some very competent. But the bad performance of the Soviet economy is usually blamed on them. Surprisingly, this attitude is popular both in the Soviet Union and the West. Only the reasons for it are different.

Two such Western stereotypes can be mentioned. One stems from thinking in terms of modeling, optimums, rational expectations, etc. The idea here is that there can exist different models of economies, and that in any of them there is always room for improvement. Therefore, if improvement is not made in the Soviet economy, Soviet planners must not possess the necessary

skills or do not use the appropriate tools. Another
stereotype results from idealizing the principle of
socialization. Those economists who favor this principle consider Soviet failure a consequence of the
distortion of socialism, and hold bureaucrats, and
planners most of all, responsible.

The discontent in the Soviet Union is of another
nature. Dissatisfied as consumers, people usually
blame planners for everything. Concerning even those
in managerial and professional positions, one must
realize that they have never studied or discussed
openly the problems that the Soviet economy faces.
This does not mean that they accept the propaganda
about the boundless advantages of a planned economy,
but the spectrum of opinions as to causes of the
problems is very broad. Facing numerous obstacles in
their work, engineers and other professionals think
that the authorities lack the talent to do anything
about the economy. This feeling is owed especially to
the notorious Communist party methods for appointing
staff (nomenklatura). Most managers and professionals
do not realize the interdependence of different economic problems and the role of economic principles. If
the principles do not work, one cannot expect that a
sage will do much better than a fool. In general, the
attitude of professionals in the Soviet Union toward
failures of the economy seems to center too much on bad
leaders and planners, etc. Even those favoring political changes, as far as we know, do not suggest positive
economic programs.

The official attitude toward the planning system is
dual as well in regard to the advantages of the planned
economy in general. The potentials are praised much
more than the reality. If the performance of Gosplan,
not to mention other planning bodies, has been criticized periodically, the leaders are proud of planning

as an institution. One may even get the impression that they are sometimes pleased that it still works. In this respect, it might be interesting to see how the system became involved with central planning and how consistent the latter is with Marxist economic theory. The role of Marxist ideology in Soviet society is well known and is described, for example, in [17]. We will approach the topic briefly from the standpoint of national economic planning.

Marxism has not produced a systematic theory for a socialist economy. Its original thought was that a socialist economy would overcome the "anarchy of capitalist production." The idea of a unitary plan followed from this as a logical consequence. Before Lenin seized power, he was little concerned as to how the economic system would be developed following a revolutionary victory. After the October revolution, however, he realized that the task of building Communism would be more complicated than had been expected. Since he did not have any economic guidelines, he decided to retain the existing capitalist organization. But, in accordance with ideological doctrine, it had to be controlled both by the government and the workers. Very soon, in the summer of 1918, this approach was abandoned. The period from that time until 1921 is known as the period of "War Communism."

The aims of the new administration were expressed in a special resolution proposed by Lenin and drawn up at the conference of Economic Councils in January, 1920 [34]. It stated that "the centralization of the national economic administration is the principal means at the disposal of the victorious proletariat for developing the productive forces of the country and securing for industry the leading role in economic life." While bourgeois governments confined themselves

to planning their budgets, the Soviet government had to
make use of sanctioning plans for the most important
branches of industry.

Gosplan was created in February 1921. It was at
this time that a New Economic Policy (NEP) was
announced (the essence of NEP was partial restoration
of the market and horizontal economic relationships
among enterprises). Gosplan developed the idea of a
General Economic Plan without which various individual
plans might come into conflict with each other. In
1925 Gosplan released an outline for such a plan,
entitled Economic Control Figures of the USSR for
1925-1926. This event was decisive in the further
development of the Soviet economy. In 1927 the First
Five-Year Plan, for 1928-1933, was constructed.

Present national economic plans have exceeded the
scale of those first naive plans. The contents of a
plan are represented in dozens of volumes, with the
tables of indicators and their values. The plan envel-
ops all stages of inputs allocation, production of
goods and services, and income distribution. It regulates all aspects of society, from the manufacture of
heavy equipment and military hardware to the activities
of prisoners and the handicapped.

In planning, the Marxist practice of classifying
all branches of the economy into two spheres -- productive and nonproductive -- is used. Branches related
to the production of material values are considered
productive, and those related to the production of services are considered nonproductive. While some
branches can be classified easily, the process is
overly complicated for others. This is true especially
for transportation, communications, and trade.
Transportation and communications serving enterprises
and organizations are viewed as productive, and those
serving the public as nonproductive. Although the

same facilities can be used in both cases, the conventional Marxist division is made. The situation is even more complicated for trade. Operations such as packing and wrapping, which increase the values of commodities, are classified as productive. On the other hand, services of salesmen and cashiers are identified as nonproductive. In this case any conventional division would be senseless. Therefore, in deviation from Marxist classification, trade as a whole is included in the material sphere. In the first few years of the 1965 Economic Reform, there was wary discussion of these issues. Some economists tried to revise the role of the nonproductive sphere in general, but the discussion was soon stopped.

Marx divided society's total production into two departments -- means of production and consumer goods -- and considered conditions for the exchange between them [26]. Corresponding divisions play an important role in planning. In all annual plans, detailed calculations have been performed for all products manufactured by industry. This is a very complicated problem though the technology used is simple. There are some goods that people cannot possess and that are used only as means of production. Some others such as cars, for example, are conventionally considered as pure consumer goods. But many other products such as electricity, gasoline, nails, fabrics, sugar, meat, etc., serve a dual purpose. The Central Statistical Administration (TsSU) releases coefficients for these products based on estimates of their use as means of production or consumer goods. Taking account of these coefficients, two special subdepartments of Gosplan divide national gross social product into the two categories in question. The precision of this work of course is doubtful.

A controversial conclusion derived from the Marxist

theory of growth is that, to provide the right proportions for the development of the economy, the first
department -- means of production -- must keep ahead in
its growth relative to the second -- consumer goods --
(although this does not follow directly from Marx's
schemes of reproduction). This "law" is considered to
be one of the fundamentals of the planned economy. But
we would say that Marxist theory has been used in this
case only to explain actual developments. If it were
necessary, an excuse could be found for violating the
principle. For example, the assertion that it pertains
only to the long run has occasionally been made. As a
matter of fact, an attempt to reverse this tenet was
made in the 9th Five-Year Plan (1971-1975). Planned
rates of growth for manufactured consumer goods were
higher than those for means of production. Unfortunately for the consumer, the attempt failed, and the
"law" held as it had before.

The period of 1965-1980 has been chosen in this
study for several reasons. It begins at the time that
the present Soviet leaders came to power and initiated
the 1965 Reform. Further, the period was full of
alterations in the organizational structure of the
economy and methodology of planning. The changes may
be more or less visible from a distance, but have an
impact on the further development of the Soviet
economy. Since, for biological reasons, a change in
Soviet leadership can be expected in the next few
years, it is important to attempt to look into the
future. A discussion of the recent state of the
planning system, the problems that it faces, and the
methods used can be very helpful in this respect.
Analyzing the evolution of the planning system, we will
emphasize its practical worth, motives for change, and
the conformity of intensions and results.

The material will be classified in such a way that

the effects of all changes are attributed to one of three possible sources: (1) the economic principles of management and fundamentals of the system; (2) the organizational structure of planning and its institutions; and (3) the methodology of planning. We find that identification of various alterations with these groups can be helpful against possible confusion. For example, both the decreasing centralization of the economy and computerization of planning calculations are considered improvements. But they are of quite different natures and may even work in opposite directions. While the former is related to the principles of the system and is intended to increase the efficiency of the economy, the latter is meant to increase the efficiency of planning itself. Obviously, requirements for better planning do not coincide with requirements for the decentralization of the economy. As a matter of fact, the current program of computerization of planning aims to increase centralization of decision making. All these issues are discussed for each of the above three sources in Chapters 2 through 4. Our conclusions reviewing the materials are made in Chapter 5. The intent of that chapter is also to draw attention to recent developments which could create a bridge between the present and the future.

The author hopes that this monograph may provide the reader a better understanding of Soviet planning. Work on the monograph, which was carried out in the summer and fall of 1981, was made possible by the support of Delphic Associates and the personal cooperation of Robert T. Crowley and Gerold Guensberg. Valuable comments and suggestions by Herbert S. Levine, who acted as editor of the project, were helpful at all its stages, especially in the improvement of the original version of the text. The editor, Barbara Dash, did her best to make the product readable. Nadia L. Kravchenko proved to be a creative typist, and Philip Rothman and my wife helped me with proofreading the manuscript. I would like to thank all these contributors.

# 2
# The Economic Principles
# of Management and
# Fundamentals of the System

## THE 1965 REFORM AND THE LATER CHANGE IN CRITERIA FOR ENTERPRISE OPERATION

It is easy to make judgements looking back at accumulated materials and facts. Now, when it is clear that the 1965 Economic Reform failed to achieve its goals, we need not discuss in detail its pros and cons, particularly in view of the availability of pertinent literature in English (see, for instance, [24]). The goal of our study is not to deny the value of this reform for the Soviet economy, even if it seems doubtful. It is rather to analyze the sequence of organizational and methodological changes in Soviet planning, tracing their ties to the fundamentals of the economic system.

The 1965 Reform was the first in a series of attempts by the present leadership to improve economic performance. As is generally known, party and government authorities believed that in initiating the Reform they could increase the economic options of enterprises and, as a result, the productivity of labor, while at the same time strengthening the centralization of management in industry. Usually only the first part of this proposition is stressed in the literature, attributable to the interpretation of the Reform by its creators and official sources. Thus the Resolution of

11

the Central Committee of the Communist Party of the
Soviet Union and the USSR Council of Ministers of
October 4, 1965 [38] explained the need for urgent
action:

> In planning too much attention is paid to
> administrative protocol, and economic methods
> are neglected. Plan targets orient enter-
> prises toward the achievement of quantitative
> results. Their independence in the develop-
> ment and choice of production methods is
> unreasonably constrained. Employees have no
> incentive to improve the operation of their
> enterprises or to utilize reserves and expand
> profitability. The accountability of enter-
> prises for violating delivery terms and for
> manufacturing products of poor quality is
> inadequate. Economic contracts do not play
> their due role in relationships among enter-
> prises, and the cost-accounting at enterprises
> is, to a large extent, only formal. Such eco-
> nomic tools as profit, bonuses, credit, etc.,
> are poorly used in planning and economic
> activity. There are essential shortcomings
> in pricing.

In our analysis, we will be concerned with five
main planned targets: production, investment, labor,
finance, and material supply. Main investment plan
targets -- investment financed by the state, capital
put into use, and new productive capacities -- were not
changed by the Reform at all, i.e., were to be determined in the plan as before. The two crucial questions
that the Soviet planning system has tried to solve in
production plans are how to select the best indicator,
reflecting the value terms of output, and to what
extent output in physical terms must be dictated by the
plan. Before the Reform, the gross value of output,
which includes the cost of unfinished goods, was confirmed as the main value indicator. This approach was
criticized for many reasons, e.g., that the enterprise
can meet the plan by producing too few products and
accumulating stocks of unfinished goods. Trying to

create reserves for the achievement of plan goals and trying to guarantee wages, managers of enterprises underestimated the volume of unfinished goods in planning accounts and overestimated it in ex-post accounts.

In order to increase the role of the demand side of the economy, the decision was made to evaluate the activity of industrial enterprises according to the sales revenue. In contrast to the estimate of gross output, in which the total output produced was included, here only those products accepted by the purchaser were taken into account. Enterprises were allowed a higher degree of freedom in selecting consumer products and adjusting their production processes to consumer demand. Thus the list of products assigned by the Council of Ministers in 1968 was half that of 1964 and included 615 items [51].

The number of confirmed indicators was reduced essentially also in the labor plan. This side of enterprise activity is usually evaluated with many indicators, particularly the number of employees, productivity of labor, and total wage bill. While all three of these were employed before the Reform, following it the total wage bill became the sole controlled indicator. Managers of enterprises had to plan the productivity of labor and number of employees independently by category in the interest of achieving the best results. That does not mean that these indicators did not have to be included in the plans. The enterprises and ministries had to compute all of them as they did before. The only difference was that the emphasis had shifted to wage funds.

Total profit and profitability became the main indicators in the finance plans of industrial enterprises. Also payments to the budget and allocations from it had to be considered. The most essential departure from the previous arrangement was that the cost of production was no longer an obligatory characteristic of the enterprise activity. For most industrial enterprises a new definition of profitability was introduced: the ratio of profit to the sum of fixed productive capital and "normed" working capital, not to costs as before. This indicator was expected to play a major part in the Reform provisions to intensify the role of profits in economic stimulation of enterprises and to increase the material interest of their personnel.

In order to increase the effectiveness of production, payments to the budget for fixed and working productive capital were introduced. This item was intended to replace other types of payments, including turnover tax. Normatives had to be established for a number of years so that a properly functioning enterprise would have profit to cover planned outlays as well as for offering incentives. The more effective the enterprise's operations, the more profit it would derive, and the larger its share of this profit (after payments for the use of capital, some fixed payments to the budget, and loan interest payments) would be. These profits were to be the source of three economic incentive funds: the production development fund, the bonus fund, and the social fund.

As for material supply plans, deliveries to enterprises of materials and equipment distributed by supervising organizations had to be approved. The role of economic contracts and material liability were to be strengthened. The 1965 Resolution announced that there would be a gradual transition from the distribution of equipment, supplies, and prefabricated materials (plany raspredeleniia) to some elements of the wholesale trade system.

Whenever changes are made in the system of indicators, it is necessary to decide which of them will be used for the evaluation of enterprise operations. There have been many attempts in Soviet economic literature to introduce a universal criterion for the performance of enterprises, but these were far from practical planning. They either failed to consider many elements of enterprise operations or recommended that these elements be weighed. But the problem of weights can be solved only theoretically. Further, what is most important, the experiments with criteria reduced the problem of the economic foundations for the effective performance of the economy to a problem of planning methodology. They created a false sense that, when the right criteria are found and the optimal plan is computed, the economy will work in an optimal regime.

The Soviet planning system employs a multicriteria approach. Depending on policy, one or another criterion is given greater importance. Usually each successive indicator introduced for such a role is declared some sort of remedy for the economy. The perpetual pattern of change is approximately as follows. Sometime after the introduction of an indicator or a group of indicators, the shortcomings become apparent and leading planning specialists begin to write memos on the subject. If the question is open for discussion, articles relevant to it appear also in economic literature. It takes a few years before changes are made (if they are made at all), and, since none of the indicators possess only advantages, the process repeats itself. The natural question is why the possible disadvatanges are not discussed a priori.

Of course there is no unique answer. When things go badly, planning authorities have to do or propose something to be done within their spheres of responsibility. The rules of the game are such that an appearance of improvement must always be produced. On the other hand, many planners try to do their best, and, since they cannot propose a change of principle (one can guess that some of them might want to), they substitute one indicator for another, believing that the shortcomings of the former are fewer than those of the latter. There is always room for hope.

From the very beginning, the hope to increase the role of the demand side of the economy by replacing the gross value of output with sales revenue was unrealistic. More will be said on this score in considering the system of material supply. For the present, we will note that purchasers have no economic rights and agree to any terms for the suppliers' convenience. They do not want to jeopardize their relations with powerful suppliers who could, by violating delivery agreements, hinder the fulfillment of purchasers' production plans. Every year the State Arbitration Committee (Gosudarstvennyi arbitrazh) examines thousands of complaints concerning broken economic contracts [3]. The injured party is always a purchasing enterprise or organization.

With the growing role of sales revenue, enterprise managers began to concentrate on goods and work which consumed materials and energy and received a large share of finished parts from cooperating enterprises. Enterprises could surpass plan targets in value while underfulfilling them in quantity. (The situation was especially beneficial to machine-building plants.) As a result, planning authorities gradually began to increase the list of products included in plans. But enterprises could still take advantage of the essential growth of prices on goods such as rolled metal, trucks, machines, cotton, etc. This growth was especially pronounced in machine building where the average price of machine tools increased just in 1975-1980 by 42.8%,

forges and presses by 28.7%, trucks by 43.7%, etc.
[12] .

As elsewhere, price growth is not welcomed in the
Soviet economy. The traditional approach to planning
is to avoid including negative events in plans even
though they take place in fact. The basis for this is
the plan "mobilizing effect" under which, e.g., by
underestimating planned prices, one will inhibit their
growth. In general, the mobilizing effect plays a very
important role in planning, and we will dwell on it
below. Since prices grow in practice faster than in
plans, the actual increase of weighted average prices
is underestimated in planned targets, and therefore
enterprises surpass their targets in money terms. As a
rule, aggregate prices (gruppovye tseny) are .5-1%
higher than those planned, and for some goods the difference is much greater [12].

There have been numerous instances of plan goals
producing results quite opposite to those projected.
For example, there was much confusion surrounding sales
revenue in energy producing industries. Enterprises
tried to sell to their customers, i.e., other enterprises, as much energy as possible, especially at the
end of a year when there was a threat of not meeting
the sales plan. A Western reader may find no fault
with this, but anyone familiar with the workings of a
planned economy will know how much waste such practices
produce. Not until the world energy crisis were urgent
measures taken. In 1974-1975 sales revenue was
abolished as a confirmed indicator for electrical power
and gas industries.

Planning authorities, gradually gaining experience,
began to change their attitude toward the main provisions of the 1965 Reform. This had been impossible
until the middle of the 1970s, i.e., after the first
honeymoon years of the Reform. It became obvious that

if one indicator was considered more important than
another, and consequently gained influence on the bonus
fund, then the values of the others took a turn for the
worse. For example, according to the 1965 Resolution,
enterprises were to plan their labor productivity and
production costs independently. But within a few years
of its introduction the new system began to deterio-
rate. The problem was that enterprises could increase
sales revenue with the result of increased material
expenditures or even wages as long as the total stayed
within predetermined limits. In any event the bonus
fund was growing.

For this reason the decision was made in 1973 to
return to the practice of employing the labor productivity indicator, measuring it in growth rate terms.
That meant stricter influence over the number of persons employed, which serves as the denominator of the
productivity indicator (the planned output targets
being the numerator). This is not equivalent to dictating employment limits since, with the fulfillment of
productivity targets and the surpassing of output
targets, the number of those employed can even grow.
That is why it was decided also to assign employment
limits for enterprises located in Moscow and Leningrad.
In spite of severe restrictions on settlement in these
and other cities, some industrial and, in particular,
construction enterprises considered to be very important obtained special permission from the Central Committee to hire workers from outside areas. That
measure was approved to create a single source of
information about the process, to increase control over
it, and to force enterprises to present well-founded
requests.

The case of production cost is more complicated
than that of productivity. Several memos by Gosplan
specialists, which I happened to read at that time,

drew attention to the problem of the rapidly increasing cost of production. To prevent enterprises from simply finding excuses and to penalize them when the cost of production was rising at an undesirable pace, the specialists recommended a return to the practice of stipulating production cost in plans. But there is another side of the problem over which those experts had no authority. That is the quality of goods and services, the well-known Achilles' heel of a planned economy. One of the reasons for not dictating cost is to encourage enterprises to include more new products, which could be more costly, in their production programs. The 9th Five-Year Plan (1971-1975) started the decade of persistent attempts to introduce policies and requirements for the improvement of the quality of manufactured products. It was not the time to return to the problem of production cost. In the 10th Five-Year Plan these trends continued and all the omissions of the 9th Five-Year Plan were to be made up for.

The alternative decision was made to intensify efforts to set norms for expenditures of materials, energy, and equipment at all levels of management, including enterprises, ministries, and Gosplan USSR. Within Gosplan, norms were to be used by departments not only in computing the cost of products of their own industries, but also in planning the allocation of their products. In the latter case, one department calculates the production use of resources which it allots to industries supervised by other departments. This applies, for example, to the department planning electrical power. It determines the output of electricity not only according to the total requests of other departments, but also according to the aggregated norms for expenditures per unit of output for all consuming industries. At the beginning of the planning procedure, all departments submit their projections for outputs. Possessing average norms for expenditures of electricity per unit of gross value of output for all industries, the department estimates the total demand and develops the balance of electricity.

Since in the process of this work material balances (material'nye balansy) and information about output in physical terms are used, the number of products whose output is confirmed in plans in physical terms has grown gradually. If one of the advantages claimed for the 1965 Reform was the reduction of centrally planned allotments of products, in the 1981 annual plan their number was almost the same as in 1963-1964, i.e., about 4,000 [51]. (By comparison, in the 1968-1970 annual plans that number was around 2,700.)

By tightening requirements for norms for material expenditures and controlling wages, planning authorities attempted to solve the problem of the growing cost of production. At first glance, such a solution does not eliminate the possibility of introducing new types of goods, as would overall cost control, because special "relaxed" norms can be used for new technological processes. As the 9th Five-Year Plan did not result in a dramatic change in quality, new goals were imposed to that end. Since 1976, the share of products in the high quality category has been planned and has become an additional indicator confirmed in the plans.

Another problem that concerned planning authorities was that of apparent "growth without real growth." The economy needs real goods and services. But any major indicator in money terms presents the possibility of choosing, within limits, the remunerative items in the controlled commodity list (nomenklatura) while neglecting others (due to variations in price growth, as described above, and to other factors as well). While output in physical terms was stipulated in plans, in 1967 ministries obtained the right to make changes for enterprises during the course of a year, after coordination of the problem with Gosplan. Before that only direct action of Gosplan could provide such changes. Finally, despite their well-known short-comings, only value indicators can be used to compare the operation of different enterprises.

THE EVOLUTION OF THE INCENTIVE PROVISIONS

In his book [6, p. 429], Berliner suggests the following generalized formula for the bonus fund planned for Soviet enterprises:

$$B = \bar{B} + W_o[k_v(V-\bar{V}) + k_p(P-\bar{P}) + k_\ell(L-\bar{L})],$$

where $B$ = the size of the bonus fund in the current annual plan,

$\bar{B}$ = the size of the current year's bonus fund as approved in the enterprise's five-year plan,

$W_o$ = the total wage bill in the last year pre-ceding the current five-year plan,

$V$, $P$, and $L$ = the current year's actual targets for increased value of output, for the profit rate, and for increased labor productivity, respectively,

$\bar{V}$, $\bar{P}$, and $\bar{L}$ = the corresponding five-year-plan targets for the current year,

$k_v$, $k_p$, and $k_\ell$ = the corresponding coefficients.

Although the formula catches the idea, some details need clarification. The 1965 Resolution prescribed that the bonus fund would be computed as the percentage of the total wage bill depending on the growth rate of sales revenue in "comparable" prices (or profit in current prices) and the level of profitability provided in the annual plan. From the beginning, difficulties arose in the attempts to introduce a unified approach, not only among different industries but also within them. The reason was the varied profitability of enterprises.

For example, in the garment industry the ratio of the profitability of the best to the worst enterprises is about four to one. Evidently, pure manipulation of prices will not eliminate such a discrepancy. Sales revenue growth in this industry depends on the quality and prices of fabrics, not on the operation of enterprises. To reduce such dependence and relevant fluctuations of the bonus fund, it was decided to compute it on the basis of total sales, not the growth rate.

At some enterprises of extractive industries such as coal, oil, and ferrous metallurgy, sales revenue may not grow at all. Special systems of incentives were introduced for those enterprises, in some cases different from the incentive systems for whole industries. In the coal industry, special accounting prices (raschetnye tseny) were computed, for this purpose only, so that they could guarantee the minimum stipulated level for the bonus fund.

In general, depending on the conditions in the industry, one of the indicators -- total sales revenue, its growth rate, profit, or its growth rate -- was used for the determination of the bonus fund, separately or in combination with the level of profitability. Even the latter was computed differently, as the ratio of profit either to the sum of "normed" fixed and working capital or to cost. The intention was to increase the bonus fund for unprofitable enterprises and to reduce its growth for those with high profitability. In the first situation, profit is usually the preferable criterion and, in the second, sales revenue.

In all cases when the method applied deviates from the basic instruction, it must be approved by the Interdepartmental Commission for New Methods of Planning and Economic Stimulation (Mezhduvedomstvennaia komissiia po voprosam primeneniia novykh metodov planirovaniia i ekonomicheskogo stimulirovaniia) at Gosplan.

The principles described were formed at the end of the 1960s. They were applied in the calculation of bonus funds in the 9th (1971-1975) and 10th (1976-1980) five-year plans. But, since from the beginning of that period annual subdivisions of five-year plans were computed, it was decided to relate bonus funds also to successes in meeting those annual targets. Therefore the above principles continued to be used only in fixing the basic yearly values of the fund in the five-year plan. The actual values of the fund however could be higher or lower than those depending on targets adopted by an enterprise in the corresponding annual plan.

Beginning from 1973, such a change in the bonus fund was calculated with fixed normatives depending on the discrepancy between the targets of the annual plan and the five-year plan. Several indicators -- the growth rate of the gross output, the level of profitability, the growth rate of productivity, the proportion of high-quality products having a special "seal of quality" (znak kachestva), and, added in the 10th Five-Year Plan, the degree of underdelivery -- determined the fluctuation from the basic value of the fund fixed in the five-year plan.

The 1965 Resolution called for increasing the role of economic contracts and the responsibility to meet them. Stricter penalties in the form of deductions from enterprises' profits were imposed, although they did not influence the bonus fund directly and, for this and many other reasons, did not succeed. Violating the "assortment plan," enterprises could meet the plan targets in total estimates, failing to meet the requirements for the quantities of goods produced. In

1976-1977 a methodology was developed for calculating the bonus fund with a delivery plan account. The provisions of the method are as follows. The operation of the enterprise is still evaluated with an indicator in money terms, but all deliveries are both totalled and counted separately. Underfulfillment of the plan in one case is not concealed by surpassing it in other cases. The quantity of an "underdelivery" measured in money terms is subtracted from the planned sales target, automatically reducing the incentive fund. The idea can be illustrated with the following formula:

$$Q_a = \bar{Q} + S - U,$$

where $Q_a$ = the actual sales revenue of the enterprise,
$\bar{Q}$ = the planned sales revenue of the enterprise,
S = the inflow of sales revenue resulting from surpassing some delivery contracts,
U = the losses in sales revenue resulting from underfulfillment of other delivery contracts.

Then Gosplan calculates only that value of sales revenue, $Q_c$, which is in accord with the planned contracts for delivery:

$$Q_c = \bar{Q} - U,$$

and substitutes the result for $Q_a$ in computing the bonus fund. Using this approach, planning authorities decreased the bonus fund by 128 million rubles in 1979, but that had little effect on delivery totals [51]. Numerous corrections to plans, changes in assortment and terms, and price growth, along with other factors, contributed to this. Planning authorities had serious problems trying to isolate cases of real violation for which enterprises could be penalized.

Some economists raise the question of why the

Soviets do not use profit as a single reasonable indicator for evaluating enterprise operations. The above
considerations demonstrate however that it does not
appear so reasonable to them. Each time that it is
necessary to improve the situation with an indicator,
direct regulation is required. For this reason, the
number of indicators influencing the bonus fund eventually grew. Different systems were introduced for
enterprises in the same industry, and rates of deductions into the bonus fund for meeting the same target
varied substantially over time [46].

A new change in the evaluation of industrial
enterprise operations was introduced by the 1979 Resolution of the Central Committee and the Council of
Ministers [44]. The sales revenue is no longer the
major indicator determining the size of incentive funds
and bonuses. Sales revenue is still dictated for
enterprises but only in annual plans, and only at the
ministry level once approval is obtained from Gosplan
USSR. Now incentive funds depend on the growth of
labor productivity, increases in quality, and success
in completing contracted deliveries. As mentioned
above, these indicators were used as criteria for computing the bonus fund previously as well. But their
role was limited to influence on the fund's growth, not
its basic value. Sales revenue and profitability were
considered more important for most industries. Since
the 1979 Resolution, labor productivity is one of the
major targets of the plan, and it is mandatory as it
was before the 1965 Reform. Corrections for planned
delivery targets are made as in the case illustrated
above.

The 1965 Reform provided a reduction in the number
of indicators used for evaluating enterprise operations
and forming incentive funds. For these purposes, the
1979 Resolution introduced two indicators -- labor pro-

ductivity and the proportion of high quality products -- but the first is the ratio of net product to the number of employees. Therefore three indicators must be considered rather than two. Further, norms for deductions into incentive funds are defined in percentage of profits. Since, at the same rate of deduction, the greater the profit the higher the bonuses, profit can be viewed as the fourth indicator influencing the size of incentive funds. Finally, since deduction rates are reduced when delivery targets are not met, there are five such indicators in all. But this does not exhaust all the possibilities. In extractive industries, for example, the output growth in physical terms is the main contributor to the bonus fund. The 1979 Resolution mentioned also other criteria such as saving material resources, profitability, reduction in cost, etc. In combination, all these indicators when applied in an individual industry may play a role quite opposite to that projected. Maneuvering within limits of a few degrees of freedom, enterprises can anticipate compensation for failures in terms of one indicator and related reductions in bonus funds with successes in others. Methods considered most suitable for each industry will be set probably in the early 1980s.

Before and after 1965, labor productivity was measured as the ratio of the gross value of output (tovarnaia produktsiia) to the number of those employed. Now the numerator of this fraction has been replaced by the net value of output (chistaia produktsiia). Its economic sense is close to the Western definition of net value added measured as net national product minus indirect business taxes. In a planned economy, the role of the latter is played by the so-called turnover tax imposed on consumer goods.

The net value of output was for a while the subject

of debate. Its supporters stressed that the sales revenue indicator, besides presenting the problem of double-counting, encouraged enterprises to produce more material-intensive goods. Many planning experts at all levels -- from enterprises to Gosplan -- objected primarily for the technical reason that it would be difficult for enterprises to compute this indicator. Indeed enterprises calculated material inputs and net value added only for direct productive processes, not for overhead payments. When direct net output calculations were introduced experimentally at some enterprises, there were problems with the distribution of overhead and nonspecified payments for various production items. Therefore it was decided to use net product as a normative indicator, i.e., to compute it on the basis of norms for the share of net product in the gross value of output [30].

The scheme of calculations is organized in the same way as for the gross value of output in money terms. The difference is that the quantities of goods produced are multiplied here not by weighted average wholesale prices, but by the net product norms fixed for each item. The scheme can be illustrated with the following formula:

$$N = W(1+k_m) + \pi_n,$$

where $N$ = the normative of the net value of output computed,

$W$ = the total wage bill of production workers,

$k_m$ = the coefficient reflecting the ratio of total salaries of managers and other peripheral personnel to wages of production workers,

$\pi_n$ = normative profit computed as the product of normative profitability and total cost net of the cost of material inputs.

The normative of the net value of output confirmed

in the plan, $N_c$, is based on N and is usually lower than the latter, with the aim of the growth of efficiency. Thus this normative is much like a price which indeed, for a planned economy, is also a kind of normative parameter. Since fuel-extracting industries such as coal, gas, and oil do not consume raw materials produced by other industries in their technological processes, they still will use gross outputs for calculating labor productivity.

At this stage, we will point out that this indicator, like others used in evaluating enterprise operations, will create problems. A serious technical problem arises because of the normative approach. Since the net output norm is an average, it must be changed continually throughout a year as goods are added or excluded from the basic product mix. Further, there is also a problem of principle. If sales volume encourages enterprises to produce material-intensive goods, the net value targets will orient them to produce more labor-intensive goods. Trying to block any such possibility, the 1979 Resolution imposed limits on enterprise employees as confirmed in the plans. But even with a fixed level of employment, the enterprise can choose to produce goods merely because they require much labor, and in this way earn a higher bonus.

## THE PRINCIPLE OF PAYMENTS FOR RESOURCES AND THE ROLE OF MATERIAL SUPPLY

Marx considered the growth of the organic composition of capital, defined as the ratio of fixed capital to wages, as an indicator of capitalist exploitation. In a planned economy, exploitation by definition does not exist, and the change in the above proportion in favor of capital is considered as intensive growth stemming from advanced technology. Rough calculation shows that for the Soviet economy this ratio increased 1.3-1.4 times from 1960 to 1978 [32]. The data in the following table characterize the growth of national income and utilization of resources in recent years [48].

TABLE 2.1
National Income and Utilized Resources

| Indicator | 1970 | 1975 | 1978 |
|---|---|---|---|
| National Income in Comparable Prices, Billions of Rubles | 289.9 | 382.7 | 443.5 |
| Productive Capital,* Billions of Rubles | 857 | 1256.1 | 1515.8 |
| Wages in Material Production, Billions of Rubles | 114.6 | 148.2 | 157.2 |
| Capital Per Ruble of National Income | 2.96 | 3.28 | 3.42 |
| Wages Per Ruble of National Income | .40 | .39 | .35 |

As one can see from the table, productive capital increased in 1970-1978 more rapidly than national income, with the consequence that the ratio of existing capital to national income grew from 2.96 to 3.42, i.e., approximately by 16%. On the other hand, the share of wages in the national income declined by 12.25% over that time. Hence the growth of expenditures of basic funds and material inputs in industry outstrips the growth of the cost of labor.

Resources are the central focus of planning. Years of observation have convinced me that the real power of planning authorities lies in their ability to distri-

---

*Productive capital is defined as the enterprises' fixed and working capital.

bute resources. All disputes about the delegation of functions among the ministries and Gosplan concerning, for example, the latter's concentration only on perspective planning stem from the problem of who will distribute the resources. Almost all resources were distributed in annual plans, prompting conflicts about short-term and long-term planning. The 1979 Resolution made an attempt to change the situation by increasing the role of five-year plans in resource distribution. We will discuss the features of various plans later.

There are many stages in the mutual adjustment of production plans and material resources. To compose a production plan, an enterprise must form an idea of the resources that it might receive. After the production plan is compiled, based on resource limits and imposed targets, requirements for resources can be determined more precisely with direct calculations. The totals of these requirements represent the demand side, and production plan totals the supply side of the economy. In such a scheme the demands are derived from plan targets, i.e., they differ from what one is used to in the supply-demand diagram. Once production plan alterations are made, coordinated and accepted at all levels of management and government, corresponding changes in derived demands follow. The result is the so-called "satisfied" demand (udovletvoriaemaia potrebnost'). When enterprises are informed as to what their actual input resources will be, they must adjust their production plans to the changed conditions. This is to be done after the planning period starts. Gradually such adjustments influence the supply of other enterprises, the result being relevant changes in their "satisfied" demands. And so the chain process goes.

The 1965 Reform introduced payments by enterprises for fixed and working capital. Previously profits from

enterprises had been siphoned into the budget in two
forms, as deductions from profits and as turnover tax
on consumer goods which was considered independent of
enterprise operations. As mentioned above, direct
payments from enterprise profits for fixed and working
capital replaced overall deductions in 1965. They were
supposed to become gradually the main source of budget
revenues, with a diminishing role of turnover tax. The
rationale behind introducing payments from enterprise
profits was to stimulate enterprises to use materials
and fixed capital with care: the higher the payments
the lower the remaining profits and, therefore, the
bonus fund. We will not go into detail here as this
approach was well publicized in the West. What is
important to note is only that the idea was abortive
from the start, and that its role has decreased to
almost nothing.

Theoretically the idea looked attractive. However
it could not work because it was impossible to balance
payments for inputs and incentive funds. Industries
make different rates of profit which depend heavily,
among other things, on prices. The 1967 increase in
wholesale prices when, for instance, the average price
of coal grew by 80% and of electrical power by 25% did
not change the situation dramatically. There were
attempts to manipulate normatives of profitability in
order to smooth differences among industries, but, as
discussed above, this was impossible to accomplish even
for enterprises in the same industry. That is why
payments for inputs could affect only poorly operating
enterprises. These however received assistance from
the budget. After making payments for capital and
forming incentive funds, effectively operating
enterprises faced large residuals of profits that they
had to pass on to the budget. Sometimes this free
residual was 8-10 times greater than payment for

inputs. What is more, there are about 30 special bonus funds for achievements in various areas, so that enterprise managers have ways to compensate for penalties.

The creators of the 1965 Reform concentrated their efforts on an incentive system for meeting a variety of planned targets. However, although it is possible to encourage careful utilization of resources, none of the incentives can take the place of economic responsibility for the use of additional resources in the production process. The crucial point is that incentives for high plan targets result only in a demand for more and more inputs.

To a certain extent, the "incentive" philosophy of some well-educated Soviet economists may stem from an erroneous interpretation of the problem of optimal mathematical programming. They applied to reality the conclusion derived from this model that it is possible to find an optimal solution subject to any constraints on resources. Much attention was paid to the investigation of possible criteria, in the belief that in this was the root of the problem. What is valid for the model never matches reality exactly, owing to the set of explicit and implicit assumptions. We would mention such "obvious" implicit assumptions as: (1) those who use resources accept risk proportionate to the profits that they want to make; (2) the market indicates real demand for goods and services that are to be produced; and (3) prices reflect, along with other problems of supply and demand, preferences of consumers. None of these assumptions is valid for the Soviet planned system. However, if the market appears to have been created through the system of material supply and artificial normative prices exist, no attempts have even been made to imitate the mechanism of risk and economic responsibility for utilization of resources in the economy. Whether the question may or may not have an answer is another story, but the fact is that the 1965 Reform did not raise it. This important point will be examined in more detail later.

The capital investment plan is a well-known illustration of waste of national resources in conditions of complete absence of risk. According to Gosplan norms, the terms of construction for most industrial enterprises do not exceed 4-5 years, from which we may derive that the annual investment in a construction project should be 20-25% of its total estimated value. But according to a Gosplan source [13], average investment per project in 1970, for example, was approximately one third of that. This means that the total of 35 thousand construction projects throughout the country was three times greater than the construction capacity of the economy. In 1970 ministries and departments moved for the initiation of more than a thousand large-scale construction projects, which are usually specified in the national economy plan, and more than 300 of these were approved by the authorities. In spite of all attempts to improve the situation, it deteriorated in the 1970s. In 1975-1979 the accumulation fund (nakoplenie), two thirds of which is used for fixed investment, increased by 12.5 billion rubles, while the unfinished construction grew by 29.9 billion rubles [48]. Such an imbalance at the expense of other items in the accumulation fund indicates that the number of simultaneous construction projects has grown, with longer average terms of construction.

Nevertheless investment is an indicator which is much easier to control than the numerous goods distributed through the system of material supply. This system was a subject of controversy prior to and in the first years after the 1965 Reform. It is known that one of the Reform's provisions was a gradual transition from the distribution of means of production to whole-sale trade. Articles describing the shortcomings of distributing goods through the system of material supply appeared even in newspapers, i.e., were accessible for popular reading, which means that they were approved by the Central Committee.

Common opinion held that such a rationing system was developed because of shortages of many products, but that the system, in turn, perpetuated those short-ages. The norms for material expenditures a priori had been overstated. Organizations supervising enterprise operations were incapable of checking technological documentation, so that Gosplan's approach to the problem was to approve norms for expenditures on the basis of actual expenditures in the previous year, with an obligatory reduction of these. Therefore, according to the rules of the game, the response of enterprises was to fix these norms at levels that could be reduced but still meet plan requirements and form incentive funds.

In the early 1970s, debate about the system of material supply ended. The list of materials whose distribution was delegated to the lower levels of management shrank, and the number of material balances and plans for the distribution of goods developed and approved by Gosplan and the Council of Ministers increased dramatically. As a result, Gosplan worked out about 2,000 material balances in the 1981 annual plan, more than three hundred of which were approved by the Council of Ministers. Ministries and departments elaborated a total of 25,000 balances [16]. What is more, in order to strengthen the role of five-year plans, an attempt was made to develop some balances and allocate the most important materials in the 1981-1985 Plan. In the 1979 Resolution, the material deliveries indicator was assigned in both five-year and annual plans. The targets for reducing norms for material resource expenditures were to be designated in five-year plans.

Liberal economists usually blame planning authorities for such developments. We cannot agree with this. If the results of the slight decentralization of material supply by the 1965 Reform had been positive, probably more decentralization would have followed. As mentioned above, the main problem of economic responsibility was not solved or even defined by the Reform. It is interesting that Solzhenitsyn has understood this better than some economists. In one of his novels, he called the economic situation in the country "obezlichka" (an overall lack of responsibility). If the system cannot work to create some risk for utilizing additional resources and nobody takes material responsibility for it, we would say that resources are safer when they are centralized. At this point of course we come full circle because the authorities in the bureaucracy who take care of resources also lack responsibility. But at least the process of decision making is dispersed among several levels, and there are many stages of control there. Some protective measures developed by the planning system will be discussed later.

THE PRODUCTIVITY OF LABOR AND STIMULATION OF "INTENSIVE" PLANS

The main methodological change in computing labor productivity introduced by the 1979 Resolution was the transition from the gross to net value of output per employee. The net value was used for this purpose before too, but only at the national and republic levels. Ministries and enterprises did not compute their net value added, and used only the measure of productivity with double-counting. Technically this is only a minor change. But the attitude and philosophy on the importance of this indicator has changed essentially over the last 15 years.

Although planners have always paid attention to labor productivity, the 1965 Reform eased the requirements for its planning and accounting. One may say that this was considered a "direct" target of control. The idea was to impose a set of incentives and to grant funds to enterprises which would force them to use inputs in the best way so that labor productivity would grow as a derivative. Also important is that, in the first several years after the Reform, the average wages per employee were not under strict control, and some enterprises began to reduce the number of those employed and increase wages and bonuses. This created two sorts of problems, political and economic. We will not discuss the political importance of the problem of employment and unemployment for the Soviets. What we would like to note simply is that the economy was not ready for such a development. From the beginning, party authorities opposed layoffs of workers, and the process was taken under the control of the Central Committee. Only a few special enterprises were chosen to conduct "experiments" with productivity, employment, and wages.

The economic implication of the growth of labor productivity with the consequence of wage increases is more interesting for our study. Paradoxical as it may seem, restricting wage increases is sometimes more important for the Soviet economy than letting production grow with increasing wages. Planners realize this in spite of the lack of theoretical justification. The usual pattern of economists' thinking is that if both output and wages increase, and the labor productivity growth level stays ahead of the growth of average wage per employee, the nation's welfare is better served. However since there are no market mechanisms that could indicate even a rough estimate of equilibrium, then generally speaking the pattern is wrong. For example, if the output of heavy industry increases sharply and those employed in it receive higher wages, but output in the areas of food and light industries and services fails to grow in the same proportion, then workers receive money that they cannot spend for goods and services. Shortages emerge, and so does inflationary pressure.

Moreover, this situation can arise even when the output of consumer goods increases. Ostensibly the trading network buys such goods from enterprises, though in fact the goods are distributed through the supply system. In this process, trade organizations may receive products that are not in demand. Because of shortages, consumers will purchase foods of any quality. But nobody can force them to purchase poor quality clothing or services. (Of course they often do not have other options.) Without further detail, we can notice that consumers may spend less money for poor quality goods than was planned. When these goods lie on shelves for years, and the prices are discounted sharply or finally written off, it adds to the discrepancy between national income distributed and national product actually used in the economy.

The prohibition on layoffs and rigid control over average wages per employee after the introduction of the 1965 Reform made enterprises reluctant to set high targets for labor productivity. In response, in 1973 labor productivity was fixed as designated in plans, and associated targets became mandatory. Then the third stage followed. The 1979 Resolution made the growth of productivity, along with targets mentioned above, the main indicator for evaluating enterprise operations and forming the bonus fund. The methodology of calculation was changed, and the normative net value added per employee became one of the major plan targets.

In the late 1960s, the Gosplan Department for the Introduction of New Methods of Planning and Economic Stimulation (Otdel po vnedreniiu novykh metodov planirovaniia i ekonomicheskogo stimulirovaniia), created in 1965, initiated an investigation of what the "intensive" plan targets for the enterprise must be. This was an admission of the failure to stimulate enterprises themselves to set high targets. Behind this step was the following rationale. Managers and enterprise employees got incentive funds and bonuses for meeting and surpassing plan targets. Nevertheless the question was to what extent imposed targets were high, and how much better enterprises could operate under other conditions.

This work got a great deal of publicity among planners and in special literature. The Scientific Research Institute for Planning and Norms (NIIPiN), which I worked for, was the major executor of the investigation. From the beginning the study took two directions. The traditional approach was to organize the overall inspection of production capacities of enterprises, which has been almost completely abandoned since the introduction of the 1965 Reform. Special inspection teams were created at the Institute, with the responsibility to develop and perform such an inspection at representative enterprises. Getting ahead of our story, we can say that this approach was at least more successful than the other one.

The second direction was scientific. A special indicator and a method of calculating the degree of "intensiveness" of plan targets had to be introduced. Research was divided into two parts, the first for enterprises and their associations, and the second for ministries and departments. The idea however was fruitless from the very start. Behind its scientific verbiage there was nothing new. The whole history of planning has been an attempt to construct and impose "intensive" plans for enterprises using one or more indicators.

Of course finding a universal indicator which could solve the problem of commensurability of different plan targets was always an attractive goal. But each time attempts failed because of the nonexistence of such an indicator. Usually the production possibilities of enterprises are measured by the degree of utilization of their installed equipment, labor force, raw materials, and production capacities which are the theoretical maximum outputs. The relative importance of these indicators is different for different industries. For those producing consumer goods the most important is the problem of raw materials. For machine-building industries, where production capacity was traditionally the key indicator, the problem of utilizing metal has gradually assumed first priority.

The investigation initiated in the 1970s attempted to replace these incompatible indicators with a universal one. Initially researchers looked for something completely new, but very soon they returned to the existing indicators, this time to seek a new way to measure them. The only problem was determining their relative weights. For instance, there were proposals to use the product of labor productivity and the coefficient of utilization of capacities, or the square root of the sum of their squares, and so on. Several times Gosplan gave instructions to experiment with calculations based on these proposals. As could be expected, all attempts came to naught. The "Instructions for Computing Intensive Plans" [29] adopted by Gosplan in 1980 is evidence of this. A summary of the "Instructions" follows.

A plan is considered "intensive" if it ensures the fulfillment of authorized targets and efficient utilization of resources. Among the indicators used in evaluating the degree of a plan's "intensiveness" are: (1) utilization of production capacities; (2) labor productivity; (3) proportion of high quality products; and (4) production cost. The degree (coefficient) of "intensiveness" is determined as a ratio of an actual value of an indicator to its normative value, and its optimal value is a unity. The criterion of "intensiveness" is usually one (or sometimes two) of the above, with the others serving as complementary. The selection must be made by the supervising organization according to the concrete targets of each industry and the specific character of its production. Also it must be taken into account that, with the growth of production capacities, the growth of output is mandatory. And this is the result of more than ten years of research.

The key to these problems of incentives and criteria are wages and their distributiuon among the employed. If the 1965 Reform stressed the importance of designating the total fund of wages in plans, the 1979 Resolution declared that labor productivity and limits on the number of employees, along with previously imposed limits on wage rates, were the most important targets of the labor plan. The policy on wage funds has been changing. The following provision was made. Wage funds must be planned not in absolute values, but with normatives per unit of output (net value for most industries). This means that, with growing output, total wages can also grow within limits [31]. Of course wage increases per employee are under rigid control, and possibilities for reducing the number of workers are restricted. Nevertheless we think that an undesirable trend of wage increases will show up in those industries which have already shifted to normative planning of wage funds. As before, the authorities will probably be obliged to impose, besides the above normatives, absolute upper limits for wage funds.

The problem of wages growing faster than the production of consumer goods was discussed above. From discussions with planners I gathered that, in the annual plan, a difference of several billion rubles between total wages and the supply of consumer goods is usual. The real effect is even more pronounced if we take into account that some goods are not sold for many years, and eventually their prices are discounted sharply relative to their costs. The accumulative effect of such a discrepancy is an important contributor to inflationary pressure in the economy.

In connection with the topic of labor productivity, let us touch on the widely-discussed problem of the insufficient work force in the USSR. By definition labor productivity can increase with the growth of output and/or reduction in the size of the work force. Party and planning authorities want enterprises to meet high productivity requirements through increased output, while enterprises would be more interested in reduction of work force if there were a possibility of wage increases. Since the latter is not the case, enterprises are not interested in real layoffs. On the contrary, when the output targets get higher, enterprises demand that employee limits be raised. There is much evidence that such demands are artificial. An officially documented case was the "Shchekino Experiment" conducted at the chemical plant of the same name. Interestingly, such explicit information was available only in the first years of the development of the 1965 Reform.

The Shchekino Experiment was initiated in 1967. The idea was simple: to meet plan targets with a smaller work force when the only restriction on wages was that their total was fixed. Although in fact the degree of freedom was not so great, the essential growth of wage rates both for workers and managers was allowed. As a result, 853 persons were laid off in less than two years [47]. No information on the relative scale of the layoff was presented, but a rough estimate of implicit data shows that this amounted to about ten percent of those employed at the enterprise. One of the preconditions was that those laid off would be hired by other enterprises, and the Ministry for the Chemical Industry was involved in solving the problem.

The results of the Shchekino Experiment were discussed and approved by the Central Committee, which indicated the importance that was assigned to the case. The Central Committee authorized continuation of the experiment at several other enterprises including machine-building plants, but this lasted only until the early 1970s. It was possible to place laid-off workers in other enterprises only in isolated experiments. The thought of such an experiment on a mass scale would be frightening. Therefore the answer to the question of whether there is a labor shortage in the USSR is, as in many similar situations, yes and no. Everything depends on the assumptions made. Under present conditions, the answer is yes. We think however that the answer should be negative for the potentialities discussed in Chapter 5.

INCENTIVES, CONTROL, AND THE PROBLEM OF ECONOMIC RESPONSIBILITY

As discussed above, there were during the last 15 years many attempts to arrive at a compromise between the economic methods of management and direct control by the central authorities. From this standpoint, the 1965 Reform was not of much help for the economy. Gradually all the provisions of the Reform began to work in directions opposite to those projected. The cause of this was not only the reluctance of party and planning authorities to put into effect all the Reform's provisions, as some economists allege. The real problem was that the creators of the Reform attempted to build a structure without a foundation. It was a well-reasoned logical model on paper but a failure in practice. Whether the Reform was a move in the direction of decentralization of the economy, as is widely believed, is another story. More will be said on this score in the next chapter.

The idea of the 1965 Reform -- to fix criteria for and constraints on inputs, develop a system of incentives, and let enterprises find the best ways to conduct their operations -- was attractive but not realistic. Enterprises will find ways to comply with directives, yet will do no more. Important here is that incentives work in only one direction, as reward for achievement. Evidently that is not enough. Managers of enterprises control vast national resources. Officially the resources belong to all people. In fact many small groups of authorities at all levels of party leadership and government are in command of them, though they take no economic responsibility. By economic responsibility we understand merely paying for resources from one's own pocket and incurring losses in the event of failure. From this point of view, it is obvious that the resources belong to no one.

We would say that the central question of the Reform was how to encourage managers and workers to operate with the feeling that the inputs they manage and use belong to them when indeed it is not so. This question is usually applied in the literature only to workers and other enterprise employees. Sometimes the opponents of the regime explain workers' low productivity as an implicit protest against the system. If the problem was only with workers, it would be much easier. Simplifying the matter and excluding agriculture for the moment, we would say that, in industries where workers must precisely carry out instructions, wage policy still works.

There are numerous examples of this of which we will mention three that are better known: (1) Every year many teams of workers voluntarily go to Siberia for summer work, often having quit their jobs. They work there 16-18 hours a day, almost without a break, earning 1,000 and more rubles a month; (2) In the coal industry, two targets for production plans are set up -- a basic one and an extra one. For the fulfillment of the former, workers receive regular wages and for the latter twice as much. This system was a remedy against sharply decreasing productivity; and (3) In some special work programs, ministries or enterprises themselves are permitted to use the so-called "for work" (akkord) system of payments. This means that a team of workers gets a stipulated sum of money when the work is completed, no matter how long is takes. Under such agreements workers sometimes try so hard that they even ignore safety regulations, and injuries often result.

Unfortunately, precise adherence to the instructions is not sufficient for the management system. The problem of responsibility of managers is a peculiar one for the Soviet system in general. While economic literature and daily papers mention numerous cases of mismanagement, reference is made only to individual managers. When something goes wrong, a person can be declared a bad manager even if he is not at fault.

Somebody is always found responsible for shortcomings, whether a director, supplier, builder, or even a minister. There must be a scapegoat. But blame is never placed on management as a whole, i.e., the system.

Surprisingly, economists do not view the problem of spending national resources in the race to meet plan targets in terms of economic responsibility and do not pay attention to it. Discussing the problem with some lawyers working in economic law and arbitration, I found that they understood the root of the problem much better than economists. An interesting article of this type was published in 1974 in the journal Planovoe khoziaistvo [45], and the case is unique in Soviet economic literature. The writer does not delve deeply into causes or derive conclusions, but he stresses that there is no personal material responsibility on the part of the managers of enterprises. Therefore they have no motivation without outside enforcement to reduce costs, investigate production reserves, introduce new technology, place personnel, etc. Further, the writer notes that present legistlation provides responsibility for material damages, but only when it can be proved juridically. Since it is impossible to connect such damages with the results of enterprise operations, the legislation does not foresee the individual material responsibility of managers. The author adds also that imposing fines on managers for failure to meet plans does not work because the managers compensate themselves at the expense of other bonus funds. Although in talking about economic responsibilty, we do not have in mind the pure juridical punishment discussed by the author, we can agree with his description in general.

In the 1970s, efforts were launched to change the formal interpretation of goals planned by enterprises.

Thus the decrease in labor productivity brought a return to the pre-Reform policy of designating productivity in plans. Undesired wage growth brought rigid control of average monthly wages. Serious problems with material resources supported a centralized approach to their allocation, a move quite opposite to the 1965 Reform's spirit. Improved quality of goods was made mandatory. The Reform's criteria for evaluating enterprise operations were altered but to no avail.

It is obvious that enterprises have continued to meet their plan targets only in a formal way. One who knows how managers, engineers, and other employees of enterprises operate would not blame them for that. Working conditions have become more and more difficult, targets for production plans harder to meet, and supplies less adequate. To satisfy plan requirements, managers often must conceal reality, misuse their authority, and even break the law. It is known, for example, that a well-trained worker paid on a piecework basis recieves his monthly "rate" even when there is no work. Production norms in construction, especially for unskilled workers, are so unrealistically high and wage rates are so low, that one task is often recorded several times in order to pay a worker a reasonable amount. The result of such activities by managers may be classified by the authorities either as a success in meeting plan targets or a direct violation. No one knows in advance. One more example. As we have seen, relationships with suppliers are very important. There are many ways to maintain their friendship, from presenting "samples" of consumer goods to outright bribery. In situations like these there is much temptation for those offering bribes, and so breaking criminal laws, to benefit themselves as well. At least, the risk that they take becomes more understandable.

As mentioned before, it is impossible to invent an
indicator that will summarize enterprise performance
and possess only advantages. The real picture is
multiform, and each indicator can reflect only a part
of it. That is why, even though enterprises seem to be
bound hand and foot, they still have enough freedom to
emphasize those indicators which will allow them incentive funds and to hide their real capacities.

Thus when the sales revenue was the main incentive-
forming indicator, enterprises were inclined to produce
more material-consuming goods. If profit is the criterion, they tend to manufacture expensive goods. With
the recently introduced net value of output, one can
predict that emphasis will be put on output of labor-
consuming products. Since the 1979 Resolution declared
labor productivity measured with net output per
employee as one of the criteria for enterprise operations, enterprises will be interested also in keeping
assigned plan targets for the number of employees at
the highest possible level. In this way they can provide some reserves for future improvements. This will
present the possibility of increasing productivity
gradually by decreasing the number of employees
slightly.

Another interesting example is the approach to production planning. Before the 1965 Reform, enterprises
received large bonuses for surpassing their plans, so
that they were encouraged to set low targets. In an
effort to discourage this tendency, the creators of the
Reform decided to use a new system for forming incentive funds using two different scales -- a higher one
for production meeting plans and a reduced one for production exceeding plan targets. According to their
arithmetic, enterprises did not have to hesitate to
accept higher targets since, at the same level of

actual output, bonuses would be larger the greater the
proportion of planned target in this output. Nevenrthe-
less enterprises began to set even lower targets. The
first reason was that setting higher targets means
acceptance of higher risk:  enterprises were penalized,
and managers punished, for not meeting plan targets.
Second, since bonuses for excess production had been
reduced, the loss could be eliminated by increasing the
volume of overproduction. The problem in this case is
to set a lower basic level of output which will guarantee the high level of overfulfillment. Therefore many
attempts were made by planning authorities to determine
the real capacities of enterprises and force them to
accept "intensive" plans. But, as discussed above, all
attempts came to nothing.

# 3
# The Organizational Structure of Planning and its Institutions

## THE BRANCH PRINCIPLE OF MANAGEMENT

It is widely believed that the 1965 Economic Reform was a move toward decentralization of the Soviet economy. There is reason however to doubt that this is true. Of the two consecutive resolutions adopted at that time -- concerning the restructuring of industrial management and introduction of planning for efficiency and economic stimulation -- Western economists pay more attention to the second. Yet the first resolution had more serious impact on the economy [37].

The first resolution abolished the territorial principle of management which had been initiated in 1957 with the establishment of local national economic councils (sovnarkhozy). The vertical branch principle of management was reestablished for industrial enterprises, and industrial ministries were recreated, in some cases from existing state committees. According to this plan, all machine-building enterprises were to be supervised directly by more than a dozen national branch ministries. Within a few years some of the most important industries, such as gas, oil, and chemical, and many large enterprises from other industries were supervised on the "union ministry-enterprise" principle. Other industrial ministries were created on the union-republican prin-

ciple, i.e., having branches in all republics or at
least in those with a concentration of supervised
enterprises. The idea was to establish dual subordination of their enterprises to the corresponding
union-republic USSR ministries and to the council of
ministers of each republic in which the enterprises
were located. But in practice the idea was fruitless
for reasons that deserve special consideration.

Not surprisingly, Soviet economists use official
phraseology in explaining important developments. The
following is the standard explanation of the rationale
behind the reorganization of industrial management
[24]:

> Reform of the system of planning and economic
> incentives in industry is inseparable from
> simultaneous restructuring of industrial man-
> agement. The national economic councils did a
> certain amount of useful work, especially in
> local production coordination, i.e., on a
> territorial level. But, at the same time,
> administration based on the territorial prin-
> ciple has also had negative effects: it has
> hindered the introduction of a single-branch
> technological policy; it has weakened intra-
> branch specialization and cooperation which
> are no less important than territorial
> cooperation; it has led to a certain irrespon-
> sibility stemming from the lack of strict
> distribution of functions among national eco-
> nomic councils and branch committees, etc.

This explanation is typical of the "Khrushchev
style," explaining everything with generalities which
have, by now, become anecdotal: "The conditions are
ripe." Our aim is not merely to indicate that the
writer was wrong. Now his words can have only his-
torical interest, but the question itself is of much
importance for the Soviet political and economic
system. It is obvious that all changes in indicators
for evaluating enterprise operations lowering the
number of plan targets and introducing incentive funds

brought about by the Reform were possible also under the territorial system of management. Two events occurred independently and with little cause-and-effect relationship between them.

The national economic councils had enlivened the country's economy since they were able to pay more attention to the production of consumer goods, building materials, housing, municipal services, road construction, etc. One of the reasons for this was that they were closely supervised by republic and province (oblast') party authorities who required their enterprises to be more locally-oriented in the production of commodities. On the other hand, these territorial economic councils complicated to some extent the coordination of large-scale national projects, such as the space program and the manufacture of military hardware, and demonstrated shortcomings in the organization of heavy industry. But a well-developed system of priorities in the distribution of resources and wages, in combination with personal responsibility of the highest local authorities for meeting related plan targets, helped compensate for inadequacies.

Since it is quite well known that the reason for the 1965 Reform was political rather than economic, we will not discuss this theme. It should merely be noted that Brezhnev's administration reversed the increase in the role of local party authorities, especially since the new leaders did not trust Khrushchev's local associates. At the same time, in centralizing control of the party apparatus it was necessary to provide adequate changes in economic management. Indeed its standing was strengthened as soon as all economic power had been concentrated in Moscow. Since the Reform, the Central Committee of the Communist Party has gradually become the highest economic authority surpassing the USSR Council of Ministers. The place of planning institutions in this process will be discussed below.

At this point, claiming that the new leadership brought economic management in line with centralized party administration, we come to a conclusion which contradicts the widespread view of the decentralizing character of the 1965 Reform. The difference in opinion stems from the fact that two events took place simultaneously. While economic administration was concentrated in some 50 ministries and departments in Moscow, the economic prerogatives of the enterprises supervised by them were supposed to increase. Which of these two provisions had a stronger impact on the Soviet economy? We consider several circumstances important in this respect.

First, although enterprises could themselves determine, in accordance with the Reform, a few of their plan indicators, the decision-making process for other indicators approved by the supervising authorities became more centralized than before. Taking into account the interdependence among all indicators, it is easy to understand the limited character of enterprise autonomy. Second, the distribution of intermediary materials, which is of utmost importance in planning, was from the very beginning of the Reform concentrated in the hands of central institutions. All-union ministries became the sole holders of funds apportioned for enterprises in cases of both union and union-republic subordination. Third, enterprises never did acquire all the rights promised them in the 1965 Reform. As discussed in the second chapter, the decision to delegate some rights to enterprises failed because no provisions were made to establish the economic responsibility of their managers and employees. Given the complete lack of economic responsibility, the striving for higher and higher plan targets to produce higher wages and bonuses led to the expenditure of more

and more national resources in the production process
without proportional impact on the public welfare. As
a result, party and planning authorities eventually
moved away from almost all the provisions of the
Reform.

For the above reasons, we believe that the primary
effect of the Reform was the centralization of economic
management, with the long-term result of economic
deterioration in the republics and provincial regions
of the country. Will Brezhnev's successors return to
the territorial principle of economic management? We
will also postpone the discussion of this topic for
later.

What is important now is to stress that the mere
delegation of some rights to enterprises is not a move
toward decentralization of the Soviet economy. Under
the existing political and economic system, in which
the managers are not affected by enterprise losses
because they are not economically responsible for them,
the distribution of material resources tends to be kept
highly centralized. All important planning decisions
will be made at the top level of management. Hence
this top level of decision making holds the key to the
problem. The idea of "the bureaucracy vs. enterprises"
is far-fetched for the Soviet economy and results from
the idealization of the situation in the enterprises.
The real question is: What is the status of the
decision-making bureaucracy?

In this respect, decentralization can be viewed as
the distribution of the economic power of the top level
decision-making bureaucracy by its branching and
dispersion through the vast territory of the country.
The national economic councils performed such a function, but of course many other models are possible.
Two conditions are important in this connection.
First, these new decision-making bodies must be close

to the local centers of production and distribution of goods and services, i.e., organized on the horizontal territorial rather than vertical branch principle. Evidently the horizontal organization of decision making can be more flexible than a sole vertical structure. Second, they must correspond to the structure of the party hierarchy which plays the leading role through the whole process of planning and management. This hierarchy is organized on the mixed vertical-horizontal principle, but decision making is strictly centralized. In the horizontal structure, local party institutions will play a more significant role than at present. Although theirs is not the best guidance, they will at least maintain some economic discipline if not complete economic responsibility. Further, horizontal party authorities would show more concern for the local population than would the depersonalized vertical structure.

## THE DISTRIBUTION OF FUNCTIONS IN THE PLANNING PROCESS

The general system of planning consists of three levels: (1) economic units in enterprises and production associations (proizvodstvennye ob'edineniia); (2) the main administrations of ministries (glavki) transformed into industrial associations (promyshlennye ob'edineniia), and the main apparatus of ministries and departments (vedomstva); and (3) the Gosplan system. Gosplan is a union-republic institution, i.e., gosplans of the Soviet republics are considered branches of the central body in Moscow.*

---

*Since the English language lacks equivalents for some Soviet bureaucratic terms, we will use the word "departments" both for the subdivisions of Gosplan (otdely) and administrative institutions such as state committees (gosudarstvennye komitety), the Academy of Sciences, sport societies, etc., which are united in planning under the name "vedomstva".

Plan construction is not the only function of the ministries, departments, and Gosplan. Supervision of the meeting of plan targets is their second important function. After the 1965 Reform, control was limited to ministries and departments. Gradually it was decided that the role of the ministries and departments was not great enough, and that the involvement of Gosplan in the regulation of the production process was important. This function of Gosplan has grown, especially in connection with new possibilities presented by the computerization of planning.

Another function of the planning bureaucracy which usually is not described in economic literature is the execution of special assignments from party and government authorities, in particular providing them with information and preparing corresponding surveys and reports. Different departments of the Central Committee and the Council of Ministers, as well as republic authorities, may need information about the introduction of computers in various industries, production of certain kinds of goods, fulfillment of construction plans in an industry, training of new workers in vocational schools, occupational injuries, fulfillment of numerous resolutions, etc.

The functionaries of the party apparatus and government officials can obtain necessary information directly from the relevant departments of Gosplan, which will prepare it in the required form and within stipulated deadlines. The information is used for preparation of resolutions, decisions, official speeches, and discussions at special conferences. Collecting and preparing this information and elaborating of corresponding reports consumes a large part of the time of Gosplan experts. On the other hand, the policy is quite different toward research institutes asking for planning information, not to mention higher education institutions. They obtain the requested information only with special permission of the leadership of Gosplan, and then only if the topics of their research have been ordered by the Gosplan departments.

Turning to plan construction as the major function of Gosplan, we will mention its three general stages: (1) establishing guidelines for a five-year plan or control figures for an annual plan (the name "guidelines" was changed to "control figures" for the five-year plan by the 1979 Resolution as well); (2) working out a detailed draft plan; and (3) assigning plan targets to executors. It is impossible to say which stage is of the greatest importance, but most decisions do involve the second one. In an informational aspect, the whole process can be viewed as one-and-a-half iterations. A full iteration includes control figures for the movement of information from the top level to enterprises and the draft plan for movement in the opposite direction. The stage of assigning plan indicators to executors can be considered as an additional half iteration.

Control figures are only rough estimates of plan indicators which must be determined more precisely at the next stage. But they are significant in the planning process as a whole because at this stage: (1) corrections are made in five-year plan targets for a specified year; (2) the main targets of an annual plan are set up; (3) the limits for employment, wages, working capital, financial funds, and other resources are fixed; and (4) the priorities for further alterations in plan targets and distribution of resources are imposed.

Ministries, departments, and republic gosplans are enlisted to participate in the development of control figures, but the real working body is Gosplan USSR. The degree of participation by others depends on the size and relative importance of a ministry or republic. At the republic level, for instance, Gosplan RSFSR takes a most active part in the development of control figures for the republic and in all other stages of planning as well. The period for developing control figures is too short. They must be computed and substantiated in the first quarter of a current year, i.e., almost simultaneously with the accounting work for the previous year. This is one of the reasons why ministries and republic gosplans can participate more actively in determining the main guidelines for a five-year period. Almost two years are devoted to the development of proposals and final guidelines for five-year plans, in periods when planning specialists are free from work on current plans.

Only the proposal stage for main guidelines of a five-year plan is free from constraints on plan targets and utilized resources. It therefore presents a unique opportunity for ministries and republican authorities to express their views on the outlook for their areas of responsibility. Yet for the same reason, they do not expect to see their proposals converted into plan figures.

Since the main guidelines of a five-year plan and control figures of an annual plan predetermine to a large extent the future values of plan targets, the decision-making process in this stage is very important. There are many intermediate step-by-step decisions made by the Gosplan authorities in the process of computation, and they influence the outcome as a whole. But the final decision making is highly concentrated in the apparatus of the Central Committee of the Communist Party whose departments supervise the whole plan development process.

While the activity of Gosplan is supervised directly by the Department of Planning and Finance

Organs (<u>Otdel</u> <u>planovykh</u> <u>i</u> <u>finansovykh</u> <u>organov</u>) of the
Central Committee, other Central Committee departments
participate actively in the planning decision making as
well. Their control of the plan targets is based on
the sector-of-the-economy or industry principle. They
include the Department of Heavy Industry (<u>Otdel</u>
<u>tiazhioloi</u> <u>promyshlennosti</u>), Department of Machine
Building (<u>Otdel</u> <u>mashinostroeniia</u>), Department of the
Defense Industry (<u>Otdel</u> <u>oboronnoi</u> <u>promyshlennosti</u>),
Department of the Chemical Industry (<u>Otdel</u> <u>khimicheskoi</u>
<u>promyshlennosti</u>), Department of Light Industry and the
Food Industry (<u>Otdel</u> <u>legkoi</u> <u>i</u> <u>pishchevoi</u> <u>promysh-</u>
<u>lennosti</u>), Agriculture Department (<u>Sel'skokhozia-</u>
<u>istvennyi</u> <u>otdel</u>), Department of Construction (<u>Otdel</u>
<u>stroitel'stva</u>), Department of Transportation and Com-
munications (<u>Otdel</u> <u>transporta</u> <u>i</u> <u>sviazi</u>), Department of
Trade and Services (<u>Otdel</u> <u>torgovli</u> <u>i</u> <u>bytovogo</u> <u>obslu-</u>
<u>zhivaniia</u>), etc.

Gosplan USSR informs ministries, departments, and
republic gosplans as to control figures authorized for
them which must be detailed and conveyed to subordinate
enterprises. After that the second stage of planning
starts. Enterprises begin to itemize the targets set
up for them, defining them more accurately and introducing amendments. They must follow the directives on
control figures and limits for utilized resources.
However changes in detail are feasible, especially
since control figures are only an aggregate version of
a plan and may contain errors, omissions, and points of
contradiction. When deviations from control figures
occur, the enterprise has to defend them to the supervising ministry which, if it approves, must then defend
them before Gosplan. The process is both sophisticated
and informal.

Enterprises would like to reduce the magnitude of
plan output targets and increase the limits for inputs.

Their motivations can include the following: (1) the belief that the demands of supervising institutions are too high; (2) apprehension about a possible toughening of the targets and decreasing of the proportion of resources at higher levels of planning; (3) the desire to have a less intensive plan, with the consequence of higher incentive funds and bonuses; (4) low expectations of a satisfactory supply of materials since experience has shown that fewer deliveries may be received than planned, or that these may be late or of bad quality, etc.

Of course the aspirations of Gosplan are quite the opposite. High targets for the "common pie" which must grow as a result of the operation of all industries require setting up correspondingly high targets for all economic units. Scarcity of all resources, together with high pressure from all sectors for larger and larger portions, must be taken into account as a second factor in the process. Gosplan experts are aware of the motivations of enterprise managers and, unable to gauge whether their reported data are truthful, are suspicious of their initiatives. The position of the ministries in this process is intermediate and therefore more flexible. While they demand that enterprises accept high targets, they are themselves responsible to Gosplan for the meeting of those targets. Hence, in negotiations with Gosplan, they usually support projections favorable to enterprises.

While the development of plan targets takes place in enterprises, work on the draft plan starts at both the ministry and Gosplan levels. The institutional structure of the latter two is designed so that they may repeat all the calculations performed by a supervised organization and oversee its activity. Since they possess only the information reported to them, they of course may use their own estimates. Important

also is that an extended system of norms is used at all
levels, which presents the possibility of repeating all
the calculations from the beginning. Another important
consideration is that ministries and Gosplan staffs are
comprised of the leading specialists familiar with
enterprise methodology, capacities, and problems of
communication in the production process. For this
reason and because of a long tradition assigning
preeminence to material production, engineers and tech-
nologists have priority over economists, who are in the
minority among the specialists of Gosplan and the
ministries.

The above-mentioned duplication of calculations and
functions at different levels of planning has an
interesting effect on the process of plan construction.
Usually a supervised organization wants to submit its
draft projections at the stipulated time for fear that
otherwise they will not be taken into account at all.
Although, theoretically, a draft plan may be accepted
without the information from a subordinate organization, this usually does not happen. The mutual verification, coordination of different versions, and
utilizing collective experience and knowledge is considered important.

Each year a special internal order concerning the
sequence and terms of the development of a draft plan
is issued in Gosplan. Analogous orders appear in the
republic gosplans. The period covered is the second
and third quarters of the year. The order regulates
the interaction of all Gosplan departments in the process of planning and indicates the departments which
will send and receive the required information. It
also defines the inputs, intermediate steps, and output
of the system.

When we refer to Gosplan as a planning institution,
we mean its apparatus. While several thousand

employees work in its departments, i.e., in the apparatus, Gosplan (the State Planning Committee) itself is
rather small. The heads of most departments are members of Gosplan, and those of the main departments are
members of the Collegium of Gosplan, as is the leadership (chairman and deputy chairmen). In the republics,
gosplans consist of the heads of all departments, and
the collegia are formed in the same way as at the
national level. Whether a head of a department belongs
to Gosplan or not makes a difference in terms of
salaries, privileges, and to some extent the decision-
making power. With the increase of the centralization
in the economy in general, the decision making has been
concentrated in the Collegium of Gosplan. The most
influential there are the deputy chairmen supervising
relevant directions of planning.

In general, all Gosplan departments can be divided
into three groups: (1) summary functional; (2) summary
resource; and (3) branch. The last group, the largest,
is organized according to the industrial branch principle (the coal industry, machine building, light industry, etc.) or sector-of-the-economy principle (agriculture, construction, etc.). Machine building, in turn,
is divided into a total of about twenty branches so
that a department performing summary functions for all
of them is required. As indicated by their names, summary departments operate on the basis of information
from branch departments. Summary functional departments perform planning calculations on the principle of
one or several plan targets for all branches of the
economy. Summary resource departments develop material
and equipment balances and plans for the distribution
of material resources and equipment. The following
structure lists the major departments that I could
recall, with some possible errors and omissions:

## I.  SUMMARY FUNCTIONAL DEPARTMENTS

1. Summary Department for the Perspective National Economic Plan (Svodnyi otdel perspektivnogo narodnokhoziaistvennogo plana).
2. Summary Department for the Annual National Economic Plan (Svodnyi otdel tekushchego narodnokhoziaistennogo plana).
3. Summary Department for the Introduction of New Technology (Otdel svodnogo plana vnedreniia dostizhenii nauki i tekhniki v narodnoe khoziaistvo).
4. Summary Department for the Introduction of Computers (Otdel svodnogo plana vnedreniia vychislitel'noi tekhniki v narodnoe khoziaistvo).
5. Summary Department of Capital Investment (Svodnyi otdel kapital'nykh vlozhenii).
6. Department of Labor and Wages (Otdel truda i zarabotnoi platy).
7. Department of Finance and Cost (Otdel finansov i sebestoimosti).
8. Department for Territorial Planning and Placement of Production Forces (Otdel territorial'nogo planirovaniia i razmeshcheniia proizvoditel'nykh sil).
9. Department for the Introduction of New Methods of Planning and Economic Stimulation (Otdel po vnedreniiu novykh metodov planirovaniia i ekonomicheskogo stimulirovaniia).
10. Department for Economic Relations with Socialist Countries (Otdel po razvitiiu ekonomicheskogo sotrudnichestva s sotsialisticheskimi stranami).
11. Department of Foreign Trade (Otdel vneshnei torgovli).


## II.  SUMMARY RESOURCE DEPARTMENTS

1. Summary Department of Material Balances and Plans for Distribution of Materials (Svodnyi otdel material'nykh balansov i planov raspredeleniia).
2. Summary Department of Equipment Balances and Plans for Distribution of Equipment (Svodnyi otdel balansov i planov raspedeleniia oborudovaniia).

III.   BRANCH DEPARTMENTS*

1. Department of Electrical Power and Electrification.
2. Department of the Coal Industry.
3. Department of the Oil and Gas Industry.
4. Department of Petroleum Refining and Chemical Processing Industry.
5. Department of Ferrous Metallurgy.
6. Department of Nonferrous Metallurgy.
7. Department of the Chemical Industry.
8. Summary Department of Machine Building.
9. Department of Heavy, Power, and Transport Machine Building.
10. Department of the Electrical Engineering Industry.
11. Department of Machine Building for the Chemical and Petroleum Industry.
12. Department of Machinery for Construction, Road Construction, and Municipal Services.
13. Department of the Machine-Tool and Tool-Making Industry.
14. Department of Instrument Making, Automation Equipment, and Control Systems.
15. Department of the Automotive Industry.
16. Department of Tractor and Agricultural Machine Building.
17. Department of the Shipbuilding and Ship-Repair Industry.
18. Department of the Radio Industry.
19. Department of the Electronics Industry.
20. Department of General Machine Building.
21. Department of the Aircraft Industry.
22. Department of Light and Food Industry Machine Building and Household Appliances.
23. Department of Building Materials and the Glass Industry.
24. Department of the Timber, Cellulose, Paper, and Woodworking Industry.
25. Department of Light Industry.
26. Department of the Food Industry.
27. Department of the Fishing Industry.
28. Department of the Local Industry and Service Enterprises.
29. Department of Agriculture.
30. Department of the Building and Construction Industry.

---

*Since the meaning of the terminology is evident here, we do not give the Russian names.

31. Department of Geology and Mineral
Resources.
32. Department of Transportation.
33. Department of Communications.
34. Department of Trade and Public Catering.
35. Department of Housing, Municipal Services, and Town Development.
36. Department of Health and the Medical
Industry.
37. Department of Culture and Education.
38. Department of Foreign Trade.

Although this list is not complete, it provides an
idea of the departments participating in plan construction in Gosplan.

There are several flows of information in this process regulated by the order mentioned above. One of
them is directed from branch to summary departments
dealing with annual and perspective planning, capital
investment, labor and manpower, costs and profits,
housing construction, etc. Its major function is to
provide empirical data on finished work. Another kind
of information flow consists of data required for computing and substantiating input demands. For instance,
we mentioned above the example that all industrial
departments of Gosplan must submit information about
their outputs to the Department of Electrical Power and
Electrification which, having norms for energy consumption per unit of output, can determine the demand for
energy in manufacturing goods and services by industry
and in total. A third kind of flow circulates among
industrial branch departments. It is acknowledged that
none of the ministries produces goods that, according
to the classification of industries and products,
belong only to one industry, and none of the industries
is concentrated only in one ministry. For example,
even a single-product industry such as coal has its own
electrical power stations and machine-building and
metalworking enterprises.

Another important example is also an illustration of the peculiarities of the Soviet economy. It appears that all the branches of the economy which are non-productive, by Marxist definition, produce some material goods. Thus the Academy of Sciences and the Ministry of Secondary Specialized and Higher Education (Ministerstvo srednego spetsial'nogo i vysshego obrazovaniia) have their production shops, the operations of which are regulated by the national economic plan. Regulated are also, for example, the output of prisons and camps of the Ministry of Internal Affairs and the output of the Societies of the Blind and Deaf, etc. Each Gosplan department with responsibilities for a specific kind of product has to account for its entire output throughout the economy. Therefore each department obtains information from each of the other branch departments for which a specified product is not in the latter's profile.

All the above and other flows of information must be verified and coordinated. When problems emerge in the process of coordination, the level at which they are resolved depends on their relative importance and degree of influence on the total result. Much of the interaction among different departments is of a non-regulated character, e.g., exchange of preliminary data. In this case decisions often can be made by the heads of relevant subdepartments and departments. In more important cases decision making is strictly centralized, i.e., it takes place at the level of the department heads responsible for specific aspects of work or at the level of deputy chairmen of Gosplan. The process of decision making is also regulated by a special bureaucratic viza ("signing-off") procedure by which every minor problem comes under the jurisdiction of one or several departments. Anyone wishing official approval for his proposal or request should obtain in

advance the consent (<u>viza</u>) of the appropriate department heads. In the cases of serious disagreement, a
problem can be resolved only at a very high level.

This process intensifies in the final steps of the
development of a draft plan. Representative delega-
tions from all ministries and republic gosplans begin
the siege of Gosplan. Day after day, ministers and
chairmen of republic gosplans, accompanied by their
retinues, arrive at Gosplan with arguments, diagrams,
calculations, and tables with the sole purpose of
obtaining more resources. Gosplan reserves a certain
amount of resources for such situations, which of
course is not enough to satisfy everyone.

Sometimes differences in projections that have to
be resolved at this stage can affect not only particular plan targets but also macroindicators as a whole.
For example, in developing the 1976-1980 Five-Year
Draft Plan, Gosplan USSR and Ukrainian Gosplan produced
different projections of population for the Ukraine.
Understandably the estimate by Ukrainian Gosplan was
higher, as this indicator influences the volume of the
consumption fund allocated to the republic. Needless
to say, the final outcome was close to the projections
of the Union Gosplan. This example illustrates also
the above thought concerning mutually independent
calculations of the same indicators at different levels
of planning, as well as the control under which subordinate institutions operate.

After the materials of the draft plan are approved
by the Collegium of Gosplan, the apparatus of the
Central Committee, Council of Ministers, Politbureau
and Supreme Soviet, the plan is official. At this
point, assignment of the plan targets begins. The
information is sent to the ministries and councils of
ministers of the republics and, finally, to enterprises
and organizations.

In planning practice much importance is paid to
this stage since major changes in plan targets and
constraints are made at the upper level of planning
after the information leaves the enterprises. As mentioned above, the informational aspect of planning can
be viewed as one-and-a-half iterations. Control
figures, the movement of information from the top level
to enterprises, and the draft plan, with movement in
the opposite direction, form a full iteration. At the
final steps of this iteration a new set of macroindicators is made up. Changes in them may be great relative
to the control figures to which all the enterprise
targets were oriented. Therefore when indicators are
assigned to executors, at the end of an additional half
iteration, they may find that these new targets look
quite different from their earlier projections.

One of the goals of this stage is to coordinate the
indicators of the macro- and micro-levels of the economy in the process of detailing plan information. The
root of all complications is the fact that plan targets
for production in physical terms are computed in the
grouped, i.e., aggregated, nomenclature and direct
calculations cover about 40 percent of all products.
The indicators given to enterprises must be defined in
detailed assortment. Of course there are no mathematical methods for deriving unique solutions to the
problem of splitting a total into its parts. While
material balances used at this as well as at all other
stages of planning do not provide such a solution, they
are however helpful in coordinating constraints on
resources, their uses, and sources.

INCREASED CENTRALIZATION AND THE CHANGE IN RELATION-
SHIPS BETWEEN THE UNION AND REPUBLIC GOSPLANS

As noted in the first section of this chapter, the
1965 Reform centralized the decision-making process in

the Soviet economy on a vertical branch principle.
Resource distribution was centered in the all-union
ministries, which gained sole control over material
and financial allocations for industries with all-union
and union-republic subordination of enterprises.
Ministries in the Soviet Union receive allocations
directly from Gosplan, and the Council of Ministers
oversees the distribution of the most important
materials and equipment.

Since the early years of the reform, centralization
has increased dramatically. The number of items
planned and distributed at upper levels has grown
accordingly. Thus while 2,700 items were listed in the
production plans in 1968-1970, the number grew to 4,000
output items in 1981 [16]. The greatest growth was in
machine building and ferrous metallurgy.

Research in planning methodology as well as organizational changes in the economy were directed toward
further centralization. Two changes in methodology
were especially important in this respect: the use of
normative methods and computerization of plan calculations. The availability of norms for expenditures of
different resources per unit of output allowed planners
the opportunity to avoid dependence for information on
subordinate planning levels. Gosplan could perform
most calculations itself, even without information from
ministries and enterprises. Computers are also helpful
in this process, particularly in combination with the
data banks which are supposed to absorb the required
information about enterprise operations. For example,
when Gosplan without the use of computers calculated
the demand for rolled metal, it was able to take into
account 2,500 items produced with this metal. With the
use of computers, more than 9,000 items were covered.

The restructuring of management by the 1965 Reform
had the greatest effect on further centralization. At

this time changes were made in the middle level of management in a campaign to eliminate extra administrative links. In 1973 the Central Committee and the Council of Ministers adopted a resolution for the transition of industrial management from the existing system to a reduced two-or-three-links system [41]. This resolution summarized the results of several years' experiments at the middle level of administration, i.e., between all-union ministries and enterprises [9]. For example, the coal industry's six-link system (union ministry-republic ministry-combine of mines-trust-mine administration-mine) was changed to a three-link system (union ministry-combine of mines-mine).

The intention this time was to reduce the bureaucracy of the middle level of management which was often used by supervising authorities for increasing their administrative staffs. For years the number of employees in the central planning and economic apparatus was under control and expansion was strictly prohibited. Ministries, departments, republic gosplans, and even Gosplan USSR circumvented the restriction by organizing special teams at the middle level of management, especially in research and planning institutes, computer centers, and other establishments that were allowed staff increases. These teams worked on various specific assignments and numerous inspections, or directly in administration.

Did the Resolution of 1973 lead to a real decrease in the bureaucracy at the middle level? We doubt that it did. Two points are important here. First, in recent practice there have been no layoffs of administrative personnel. Instead, a universally employed term, "relative staff decrease" (uslovnoe vysvobozhdenie), is used in the sense that more work has to be done with the same number of employees. Second, during reorganizations management is declared to have become more "consolidated." In the coal industry example, above, the middle link of management, i.e., combine of mines, absorbed the eliminated trusts and mine administrations. So employees were not laid off but redistributed among organizations.

The same approach was used to create industrial associations corresponding to various branch main administrations of ministries (glavki). After the reorganization their leaders appeared to have become the top level managers of the union or republic industrial associations consisting of production associations and enterprises. The idea here was to introduce cost accounting to main administrations and to exchange their supervisory role for one of direct involvement in productive units of the economy.

The real effect of restructuring the middle level of management was the further centralization of both industrial management and decision making. Many republic branches and administrations of union-republic ministries were eliminated, with a resulting increase in the distances between enterprises and their supervising organizations. Considering also the highly centralized control of resource distribution, it follows that enterprise managers had to take frequent long trips to discuss each minor problem with their supervisors.

Actually the 1965 Reform brought a spiralling increase in the number of business trips, and such travel became a characteristic part of Soviet life. The usual direction of travel was from outlying districts of the country to Moscow. While increased centralization was the main cause of the rise in business trips, the human factor should not be ignored. Travel to the capital afforded opportunities to buy foods and goods short in supply, and so reasons for

many of these trips were invented.
The problem became so serious that numerous decrees and orders were issued to restrict the time and money spent on these trips. In 1973 the Central Committee adopted a resolution in which it was noted that more than 1.5 million people a year had travelled to Moscow on business [40]. A stranger to Moscow could get the impression that this must be a daily estimate. This estimate however reflected only the number of persons while many of them made several or more trips each year. Most important is that the ministries and departments were reluctant to reveal the true extent of this type of travel. The resolution noted that business trips had been used for personal reasons at society's expense and were a hidden form of theft of government funds. However one could hardly believe that this resolution would change the practice very much.

As a result of steps to further centralize the economy, the role of republic gosplans in decision making shrank, and the relations between them and Gosplan USSR changed. To a certain extent a republic gosplan plays the role of a ministry since Gosplan allocates material funds to all-union ministries and the councils of ministers of the republics, i.e., they are at the same level in the hierarchy. The republic councils of ministers control these funds only for the republic economic units that are subordinate to them. Republic gosplans represent their respective councils of ministers in planning and distribution of material funds.

By economic units subordinate to the council of ministers of a republic we mean the following: (1) industrial enterprises of local industry (mestnaia promyshlennost'); (2) industrial enterprises and shops of "nonproductive" branches of the economy; (3) agriculture and forestry; (4) part of the construction industry; (5) automobile and river transportation; (6) part of communications; (7) trade, public catering, territorial organizations of material and technical supply, and state procurements; and (8) branches of "nonproductive" services. It follows from this list that only one industrial ministry -- the Ministry of Local Industry -- is subordinate to republic planning authorities.

All the enterprises of the oil, gas, chemical, and machine-building industries are subordinate to all-union ministries. With the exception of the Ukraine, coal industry enterprises are also subordinate to the all-union ministry. According to statute, such industries as electrical power, metallurgy, timber, paper and woodworking, construction materials, light industry, and food processing are of union-republic subordination. However, since the 1965 Reform many important enterprises, organizations, planning and research institutes, and even branches of these industries have been transferred to the direct subordination of corresponding all-union ministries.

What are the relationships between the all-union and republic planning and managing authorities in view of the threefold character of the entire economy? There are many authoritative sources in the West that describe these relationships (for example, see [5] or [20]). Western economic literature seems to take the clearest view of the situation concerning the all-union industries. In studying economic and organizational problems, Western analysts are guided by official Soviet literature, and first of all by legislative acts. Yet these acts reflect only the facade of the structure and reveal little about planning practice. Various directives, decrees, instructions, and memos play an active role in the planning process.

For instance, according to the planning laws adopted during the 1965 Reform, the republic councils of ministers could revise the plans of all-union ministries if they were found inadequate. These laws were not phrased in precise terms. However, from the order concerning the sequence and terms of the development of a national economic plan, we can gain more understanding. It appears that republic authorities are to submit comments on the all-union ministries' draft plans. Since the republic gosplans analyze these projections and comment upon them only after their completion, it is clear that their criticism has no effect at all on the decision-making process.

At the same time, enterprises and organizations of all-union ministries are not as extraterritorial as they seem, for the following reason. While the economic bureaucracy is organized on the vertical principle, the party hierarchy involves horizontal local institutions: district, city, and province, not to mention republic committees. An interesting detail is that these institutions deal with enterprises and organizations at the administrative level, i.e., address directly to the directors of enterprises and organizations, not to the functionaries of their primary party organizations. A local party secretary's request for sending employees to work in agriculture, to clean up streets, participate in public events, etc., becomes a command for an enterprise director, particularly for the director of a small enterprise. When such a command is tied to a service for a local area, then materials, labor, and other inputs are required from the enterprise.

Meeting all the demands of party authorities occupies much of the time of enterprise managers and their staffs. Naturally they consider these demands an obstacle to fulfilling their own direct duties. On the

other hand, provincial cities and towns received almost
no centralized capital investment at all during the 9th
and 10th five-year plans. Their roads, sewage systems,
housing, municipal services, etc., have been in need of
much improvement. Therefore party authorities'
requests, which enlist enterprises to help in solving
urban problems, are beneficial to the population. At
present there are no other authorities who can force
the bureaucratic apparatus to pay attention to the
needs of local consumers.

The most controversial situation arises when the
union-republic industrial ministries have republican
branches. Some of these, for example those concerned
with food processing or light industry, have branches
in all the republics, while other ministries have
branches only in republics with heavy concentrations of
their enterprises. In cases in which there are only a
few of a certain type of enterprises in a republic, the
industrial or production associations are subordinated
directly to the respective union ministry in Moscow.
Before the 1973 Resolution on the restructuring of the
middle level of management, there were appropriate
administrations or main administrations of these
ministries in the republics.

It is customary to consider the union-republic
industries closer to republic than to all-union
industries. Indeed in reporting aggregate republican
data other than investment and material funds, union-
republic are grouped with republic data, but all-union
data are reported separately. However this does not
indicate the sovereignty of the republics over union-
republic industries. Even though the 1965 Reform
explains that the latter are of dual subordination --
to the union ministries and the councils of ministers
of the republics -- such a principle could not be
effective in planning at all.

A well-known plan requirement is that plan targets and resource funds must be associated with a particular supervising institution (<u>adresnyi</u> <u>kharakter</u> <u>plana</u>), here with either a ministry or the council of ministers of a republic. Since union ministries are the holders of the investment and material funds for union-republic industries and allocate these funds to their branches in the republics, the branches must follow the directions of the union ministries. There is a relevant proverb: "He who pays the orchestra orders the music."

Again, as is true for national enterprises, the party hierarchy's involvement upsets the picture. Moreover, if machine-building enterprises interact with party institutions only at the local level, union-republic ministries do so at the republic level as well when their branches are present there. This changes the basic pattern because republic party authorities can influence decisions for an industry as a whole. The degree of influence depends upon the industry, and there are differences among them.

The dependence discussed above is quite minor with ministry enterprises that have strategic value -- such as coal or ferrous metallurgy -- and the connection between these enterprises and republic economies is not strong. Republic officials have often complained about a lack of attention of the part of these ministries [27]. For example, the Ministry of the Coal Industry of the Ukraine may not hold to the terms for submitting draft plan materials to Ukrainian Gosplan even though the terms are fixed by the republic's council of ministers. The materials, along with the completed draft plan, can be delivered to Kiev by ministry officials on their way from Donetsk to Moscow. Since the terms of work are the same for both the ministries and the council of ministers of each republic, Ukrainian Gosplan does not have time to analyze the ministry's projections.

Other ministries, such as those for food and light industries, cannot take similar liberties with regard to republican authorities. Their agriculture, transportation, and trade and distribution ties to the councils of ministers of the republics are much stronger than those of the above ministries. They depend also on local sources of raw materials and construction materials since their limits on centralized investment are very low. Therefore these ministries have to honor the directives of republic party and economic authorities, and must cooperate with republic gosplans.

The final division of this threefold economy is comprised of the local industry and the above-noted "nonproductive" enterprises and organizations subordinated to the republic councils of ministers. Let us ask an unexpected question: Is there full republic sovereignty over this part of the economy? The answer is by no means positive.

National economic plans have a goal-oriented character (tselevoi kharakter). Simply put, this means that from the very beginning plan control figures indicate concrete targets and directions for inputs spending. For example, investment control figures received by a republic are not provided only as totals that can be spent by the authorities in ways they decide are the most beneficial for the welfare of the public. These limits form an initial plan scheme and are separated into branch targets specifying the type of capital that must be utilized as a result of investment. Republic gosplans are guided by these directives. Some changes are possible, but they have to be justified and coordinated with the top planning level.

The following question emerges as a result of this: Are republic planning institutions necessary at all if their participation in decision making is so limited?

The official view is that the purpose of republic planners is to provide substantiated projections within the
limits of their responsibility. Such projections are
considered at the top level and then accepted or
rejected. If rejected, an alternative will be offered,
and republic authorities can express their opinions.
Sometimes objections are taken into account, but often
this is not possible since they are accompanied by
demands for additional investment and material
inputs.

It is interesting to note that a special slang has
come into use reflecting the attitude toward republic
planning authorities. Economic units subordinated to
republic institutions become part of "the economy of a
small Sovmin (council of ministers)" as distinct from
the USSR Council of Ministers. When the politbureau of
a republic communist party approves a set of projections, it is referred to as a "draft" since republic
officials emphasize that their responsibilities do not
include making final decisions. Further, a production
plan summarizing the total output of a republic economy
is called a plan for "enterprises located on republican
territory" (predpriiatiia raspolozhennye na territorii
respubliki).

Is there dissatisfaction with the existing
situation? Here we have in mind not the consumer with
complaints of shortages, but the planning authorities
themselves. I have great respect for the professional
abilities of many of the planners I knew personally.
While these people are communists, it should be kept in
mind that communist party membership is necessary to
gain such positions, at least for the principal experts
and subdepartment heads on up. And while better
salaries and extra privileges (special hospitals and
clinics, restricted food and consumer goods stores,
resort facilities, etc.) encourage the recipients to

resist changes in the status quo, these same plannning authorities do have a responsibility to uncover problems and inform the leadership about them. In this connection they write numerous memos revealing actual conditions in various regions and branches of the economy, although these materials are often classified and never released to the public.

The following are several examples of such memos drawn from the Ukrainian Gosplan which I read in the 1970s. The Department of Agriculture (Otdel sel'skogo khoziaistva) complained about transporting food products out of the republic and further noted the low level of food consumption, relative to the rest of the country, in its industrial areas. The Department of Municipal Services (Otdel kommunal'nogo khoziaistva) reported that the water supply in the Donetsk Basin and other areas was poor, and that many cities and towns had inadequate sewage systems. The Department of Housing (Otdel zhilishchnogo khoziaistva) mentioned the chronic shortage of new dwellings arising from repeated failures to meet plan goals. All of these memos were signed by department heads, and we can again emphasize that it is these department heads and their staffs who must throw light on the real situation. However it is impossible to say how much is done out of a sense of duty and how much from a genuine desire to solve serious problems.

## PLANNING AND THE ROLE OF PARTY AUTHORITIES IN THE DECISION-MAKING PROCESS

We would like to distinguish two changes in the Soviet national economy that have gained prominence in the Brezhnev era. These are centralization of decision making, and the role of party institutions in economic life.

As demonstrated above, centralization took the form

of successive organizational changes in the economy.
First, the 1965 Reform brought back the vertical branch
principle of management. Then, the 1973 Resolution concerning restructuring of the middle level of management
and many other directives, instructions, and decrees
delegated major rights in decision making to the very
top level with respect to plan targets and distribution
of resources. Local territorial problems have been
neglected, and the rights of republic planning and economic authorities have shrunk dramatically. In
general, the process has meant reinforcement of the
military industrial complex at the expense of the consumer goods sector which gravitates toward and depends
on local sources of supply and distribution.

The influence of party institutions on the basic
operation of all Soviet enterprises and organizations
is well known. The notorious principle of party
control of the administration of enterprises and organizations (partiinyi control' za rabotoi administra-
tsii), which had been eliminated by Krushchev,
flourished again after his removal. Party comittees
participate in solving all administrative problems.
What is more, specially appointed "party informers"
operate openly, although without publicity. Though not
committee members, they participate in all party committee conferences and in other activities of party
organizations. They are responsible for "informing"
the supervising party authorities as to general sen-
timents and individual attitudes in organizations, and
so forth.

In planning and economic institutions, which are of
great importance in Soviet society, the role of primary
party organizations is much greater than average.
Since employees there usually are chosen from among
enterprise managers and engineers, they join these
organizations as communists. Membership in party orga-

nizations is very high and can include 50 percent or
more of the employees. All serious planning and management problems, not to mention ideological ones, are
discussed at monthly party meetings which are carefully
planned and for which speakers are carefully selected.
Party secretaries for these institutions are appointed
at the level of the Central Committee secretaries, and
by Brezhnev himself. Party committees are very powerful, and generally two of the most important administrative functions -- hiring and promotion -- are almost
completely their responsibility.

It is worth mentioning in this connection that special directives concerning hiring policy, for instance
toward minorities and ethnic groups in the republics,
rarely circulate in writing. High-level administrators
and party secretaries are instructed orally on these
points usually in central party committees. Although
the secret party mail system is used for the many special instructions that the Soviet people and therefore
Western correspondents must not discover, widespread
opinion holds that no incriminating materials are
included in them. Since Stalin's era even party functionaries discuss many problems more openly, and there
is a threat that sooner or later the truth may be
disclosed. But this topic is beyond the scope of our
study.

When we talk about party involvement in planning
and management, we mean in the first place the system
of administrative party institutions, from district
party committees (raionnye komitety partii) to the
Central Committee of the Communist Party. They, and
not the functionaries of primary party organizations,
really stand above the economic administrative apparatus. If we compare two hypothetical leaders, party and
administrative, of the same rank but at two different
levels, let us say enterprise and city, their relative

significance in the ruling hierarchy varies according to the level. While the director of an enterprise is usually top administrator, a city mayor ranks significantly lower than the secretary of a city party committee.

Planning organizations must acknowledge the instructions of party authorities at all levels, and must coordinate plan development as well as all intermediate and final results directly with the Central Committee in Moscow and the republics. Their general activity is supervised by the Department of Planning and Finance Organs of the Central Committee while plan development comes under the guidance of all other departments of the Central Committee, according to the area or direction of the plan.

The significance of the Department of Planning and Finance Organs in the eyes of Gosplan officials is that this department can open or close positions and determines appointments and promotions. The procedure, though never complete, may be desribed as follows. The leaders of Gosplan as well as other organizations are asked to choose "reserve" candidates for eventual promotion, taking into account plans for retirement and possible new openings. Primary party committees are the most active in this process.

Candidates for high-level positions such as heads of subdepartments or departments must have impressive work experience in the productive sphere, i.e., at enterprises. Bureaucrats without production experience usually do not advance very far. There are different upper age limitations depending on the position; the higher the position the higher the limit. As a rule, candidates for high positions are males, but exceptions are possible. Active participation in the party organization is necessary, and previous work experience in local administrative party institutions is a great advantage. We will not discuss here requirements of social origin, nationality, marital status, morals, etc. The list of candidates must be approved by the Department of Planning and Finance Organs. Although these appointments are important for candidates, they are only preliminary.

When a senior position opens, the chairman and the relevant deputy chairman of Gosplan choose one or several candidates from the reserve list and propose them to the Central Committee for consideration. The influence of the head of the Gosplan department in which there is an opening depends on his position in the leading hierarchy. As said above, the most influential are those who belong to the Collegium of Gosplan. After one of the candidates is approved pre- liminarily by the apparatus of the Central Committee, the nominee is considered successively by the Collegium of Gosplan, the appropriate department and the deputy chairman of the Council of Ministers, again by the Central Committee and, finally, by one of the Central Committee secretaries. In the event that the candidate is rejected, which if it occurs is most likely at the final stage, the procedure is repeated, sometimes at an accelerated rate. These are just examples of possible situations. Many high level positions are filled by specialists from outside Gosplan. The leadership of Gosplan may or may not be informed in advance, depending on the rank of a position. The highest of them -- deputies to the chairman, department heads -- are usually appointed directly by the Central Committee.

In general, there is nothing new in the fact that party authorities appoint figureheads and control all the operations of planning institutions. What is new in the last decade is the change of the roles of government and party institutions in the economic life of the country. The significance of the Council of Ministers, which had increased greatly in the first years of the 1965 Reform, has diminished dramatically along with the unreasonable expectations connected with the Reform. The time has come for discipline, and the party authorities are the only force that high-level administrators fear.

As a consequence, one can get the impression that Gosplan has become more attached to the Central Committee than to the Council of Ministers, though this is not formally true. Its interaction with all the departments of the Central Committee responsible for development of the economy has become direct and informal. Each department of the Central Committee consists of sectors supervising various kinds of activities. Without approval of the appropriate sector, it is impossible to make any serious planning decision. This does not mean that planners do not make decisions. Guided by the requirements of the Central Committee, they must be creative in finding ways of improving the economy. The apparatus of the Council of Ministers also supervises the Gosplan operations, but it pursues a policy that is coordinated with the Central Committee.

One can imagine that the departments of the Central Committee may be subject to conflicting demands for plan targets, for example, such as consumer goods and military hardware. Probably it is true, but from the beginning leaders fix the control figures so that each department sees its limits. The role of Gosplan in this process is preparation, along with substantiated proposals for the growth of the economy, of limits for investment, capacities for the production of raw materials, etc. The proposed control figures may be considered several times by the leading administrators of the Central Committee, with subsequent corrections by Gosplan, until they are found satisfactory.

The confirmed control figures indicate to all party, government, and planning authorities the new economic priorities. Although planning and economic organizations follow these priorities in setting up plan targets and resource distribution, there is some freedom in their interpretation. For this reason, the resulting draft plan is an indicator of the influence of relative forces in the economy. After a plan has been approved and a planned period begun, the recommended priorities continue to function. In an article published in 1976 in the journal Planovoe khoziaistvo, the Minister for Light Industry, Tarasov, described the impact of official priorities on his industry [49]. His complaints follow in brief.

As of January 1976, immediately after the close of the 9th Five-Year Plan, only slightly more than half of the 520 items of technological equipment planned for the industry had been manufactured. Delivery plans had not been regularly met. Only 70 percent of needed spare parts had been supplied, and the number of measuring instruments was insufficient. There had been difficulties in obtaining both cotton and flax, especially of good quality, as well as wool, synthetics, dyes, etc. The optimistic title of the article was "Efficiency and Quality are the Main Directions of the Growth of Light Industry."

In plan targets, party authorities pay much attention to the "mobilizing effect." The idea is that the targets should be high enough so that, to meet them, enterprise managers will be forced to utilize reserves in the expenditure of inputs and organization of production. This is not to say that party leaders want to promote unrealistic plans, but that for reasons discussed in the second chapter, i.e., the lack of economic responsibility, they do not trust management as a whole. Planners are to construct plans on the principle that targets should be higher than managers would set themselves. The following is an example of the above. The sector which I headed had developed a forecast for the republic's economy in the 1976-1980 five-year period. According to the forecast, Ukrainian agriculture could not grow by more than 16-18 percent during that period, in contrast to the 25 percent proposed by the republican draft plan. I discussed the results with the assistant head of the Summary Department of the National Economic Plan (Svodnyi otdel narodnokhoziaistvennogo plana) of Ukrainian Gosplan. With high professional credentials, he was in my opinion one of the best economists there.

He rejected our results. (On this point, I can say from my experience that qualified planners, who perform detailed calculations for many years and know all the various branches of the economy, do not need econometric methods to derive an accurate projection for the growth of agriculture.) The general idea behind his objection was that, even if I were right, such low growth could not be either justified or accepted. The growth rates had to follow the demand of the national economy and population. Forecasts must not be passive and should be adjusted to the high economic requirements.

Of course we do not claim to give a complete explanation here of why Soviet plans are unrealistic. We have discussed just one aspect of the problem. Our purpose is to show that when Western analysts, in line with official Soviet arguments, blame Soviet planners for shortcomings in the economy, they are not correct. Under the above conditions those who do not meet plan targets simply fail, but those who predict such failures by reducing plan requirements to a realistic level work against the mobilizing principle pursued by the party leaders. That is why negative tendencies, such as growth of material expenditures or fixed capital-to-output ratios, cannot be included in projections even though they are inevitable. It is much safer to find reasonable excuses after the fact.

The head of the Department of Light Industry of Ukrainian Gosplan lost his job as a result of a situation like that described above. He did not follow the instructions to raise the growth rate for his industry in the 1976-1980 Five-Year Plan. Probably he could not find the means to substantiate the high growth rate demanded, and hoped to prove that the department's 20 percent projection was the maximum possible taking into consideration the lack of raw materials. It may be that there were other failures among his previous activities. The discontent of the leadership is usually of a cumulative nature, and high-level administrators are not dismissed just for one mistake. Yet nobody knows which mistake may be the last.

In our discussion we have not wished to give the impression that planners are always right and party authorities always wrong. We would not venture such an oversimplification, but have tried to view the situation mainly from the planner's standpoint. Undoubtedly it is possible to look at the matter from the other side, but this is beyond the scope of our topic.

# 4
# The Methodology of Planning

## MAJOR RELATIONSHIPS AMONG INDICATORS

As we have seen, there are three stages of planning: (1) control figures; (2) draft plan; and (3) the assignment of indicators to executors. Their flows differ with respect to direction, purpose, content, and the degree of aggregation. The purpose of the first stage is to determine aggregate guidelines for all economic units with the use of hypotheses, assumptions, and goals established through a normative approach. The second stage resembles a pyramid with detailed information at the bottom and flowing toward the top where it is aggregated in such a way as to satisfy the constraints of the first stage. The third stage is mainly movement in the opposite direction along the pyramid, when corrections must be made at the bottom to correspond to changes at the top.

There are essential differences between calculations for aggregate control figures and those for a detailed draft plan. The procedure for developing control figures has an iterative character due to the fact that industrial variables which start the sequence of calculations depend on the output of the system as a whole. In other words, all economic units of the system need to consider the limits on resources which may be allocated to them. However the approximate output of the system must be found and resources resulting from it distributed before the sequence of calculations can begin. Further, initial output figures are corrected, and on the next iteration corresponding changes made in the values of all indicators.

To perform calculations at the control figure stage, then, constraints on major inputs -- labor, investment, and materials -- must be considered. But ordering and distributing material resources is a per- petual process which begins before and ends after the production plan is approved. For this reason constraints on material resources are virtually ignored in calculating control figures. This practice produces many complications and the need for numerous correc- tions at other stages.

To arrive at control figures for industry and regional units, anticipated limits on labor force and investment are necessary. While distribution of labor among various branches of the economy is determined on a territorial basis, investment is allocated on the vertical branch principle. Ministries, departments, and republics are unable to develop plan targets until all such information is available.

How are limits on resources determined at the aggregate level? The key indicator here is labor pro- ductivity which must grow even when prospects seem doubtful. But the "mobilizing effect" of plans requires that productivity be planned at a level higher than its reasonable value. The gross social product (valovoi obshchestvennyi produkt) is arrived at on the basis of the anticipated value of labor productivity in the current period and the estimate of its growth in the planned period, along with an estimate of the size of the work force provided by the aggregate balance of manpower (balans trudovykh resursov).

Although production functions are used in Soviet

econometric research, they are not employed directly in planning calculations since Marxist economic theory considers labor to be the sole source of net value added. Because of this, capital does not participate in evaluations of the gross social product. But since capital must nevertheless be taken into account, the following circumvention is used. The growth of labor productivity is computed, along with other factors, on the basis of the growth of capital per worker (fondovooruzhennost' truda). Thus these two-part calculations provide an estimate of the gross social product resulting from the growth of both labor and capital.

The aggregate balance of the gross social product splits the latter into material expenditures, which are the sum of material inputs and depreciation payments, and national income. The estimate of material expenditures per unit of gross social product in a current year becomes the basis for a projection for a planned year. Each year unsuccessful attempts are made to decrease the total growth of material expenditures, particularly in agriculture. With attention to corrections for the current year, the net value added is computed.

At the stage of utilization, national income is divided into consumption (fond potrebleniia) and accumulation of state enterprises and organizations (fond nakopleniia). To a large extent, the estimates are based on the proportionate size of these funds in the base (previous) and current years. This task is accomplished with the help of the aggregate balance of national income. At this step, fixed investment can be separated from other types of accumulation such as growth of working capital and reserves.

Unlike a free-market economy where intended investment depends on personal and business savings, planned economic theory does not recognize the role of personal savings in the investment process. These are considered merely postponed consumption to be spent in the future, most likely for durables and services. State financing of the economy and enterprise profits retained for development are the sources of investment. These sources are planned in keeping with the production capacities of the construction industry and industries producing equipment and materials for new enterprises, i.e., at the level of capital goods production. While planned savings are supposed to equal investments, in practice they usually exceed them because construction and industrial suppliers fail to meet their plan targets.

When the level of production of capital goods is determined and total limits on investment are computed, investment funds are allocated to the various branches of the economy with instructions on how they are to be used and outlines for the most important building projects. The system of priorities, with its many constraints, begins to work. For example, the past pattern of investment distribution among industries substantially influences planning decisions unless general changes in economic policy are made. The existence of many unfinished construction projects (perekhodiashchie stroiki) increases the inertia of the process since in theory they must be given first priority for investment funds.

The system of priorities too has its fluctuations, and it is hard to gauge precisely the relative importance assigned to various economic goals. Probably municipal services, including water supply, sewage, etc., and urban development problems are of lowest priority. Local party and government authorities are asked to assist in these areas with their own investment sources such as profits from lotteries, free services of military personnel, and free labor of citizens on weekends (kommunisticheskie subbotniki), etc. Medical facilities and public transportation and communication systems are also low on the list for investment, except for a few favored cities. Housing and children's day care facilities seem to have higher priority since these are considered important for keeping workers on the job. Funds for these purposes are allocated directly to enterprises which administer housing and day care within stipulated limitations.

Among nonproductive services, science, which is viewed as a factor of growing productivity, is one of the highest priorities. There are two sources of research financing: funds from enterprises and ministries, and the state budget. Financing by enterprises and ministries of scientific and experimental work is very extensive and, in accounting, is included in the cost of production. The state budget finances important applied research. The increasing role of ministries and departments in the distribution of these funds means further centralization of management of applied research at enterprises.

To obtain funding for any type of research, a project must prove its positive potential effect on the economy with calculations of efficiency (ekonomicheskaia effektivnost'). Substantiations of this kind are commonly invented. Unfortunately, even this tactic is of little help with fundamental research in medicine, biology, theoretical mathematics, etc., which are not considered essential to the achievement of particular economic goals.

The order of priorities among industries is well established. For years, light industry and the food industry have received the smallest investment funds. But even these sums have not been completely utilized. Of the many reasons for this, one is that production by agriculture of the raw materials demanded by these industries has not kept pace with their planned expansion. This is true even though, as is well known, agriculture has very high priority.

Finally we come to the military-industrial complex, which includes branches of machine-building and other industries dedicated in part or whole to the production of military hardware or the supply of raw materials, energy, and semifinished parts to be used in such production. Among these industries are aircraft, defense, electronics, radio, general machinery, medium machinery, and shipbuilding, along with producers of precision instruments and other control and measurement devices.

In addition to the above machine-building branches which specialize in the production of military hardware, all other machine-building industries fill special orders (spetszakazy) for the military complex. These include, for example, producers of machinery for building and road construction, and the automotive and chemical industries. Special military orders are welcomed by enterprises and design institutes to whom they mean higher wages, additional bonuses, lifting of wage growth limitations, additional funds for housing, hiring of better-qualified personnel, and so on.

With all this investment in military production and heavy industry, it is impossible to develop sufficient capacities for producing consumer goods. Because of this, "defense" enterprises are obligated to manufacture also toys and cigarette lighters, hardware and home appliances. The higher-quality resources are designated for military hardware production, and what's left over is for consumer goods. Indeed the original purpose of manufacturing consumer goods at military enterprises was to utilize wastes of technological production. Eventually special bonuses, varying with time, were established to stimulate consumer goods production at military enterprises.

Once limits on investment and labor are allocated to ministries, departments, and republic gosplans, these economic units can perform the sequence of aggregate planning calculations. Figures on their main targets are issued to them as well, even though these may be computed on the basis of announced resource limits. Now the second stage -- the draft plan -- begins.

Of the roughly 20 targets in a draft plan, the major ones are:

1.  Main indicators (balance of the national economy, effectiveness of material production, and indicators of complex plans for republics).
2.  Industrial production by branch.
3.  Agriculture.
4.  Forestry.
5.  Transportation and communications.
6.  Capital construction (investment, construction, and projection and surveying work (<u>proektno-izyskatel'skie</u> <u>raboty</u>)).
7.  Geological surveys.
8.  Scientific research and the utilization of technological advance by the national economy.
9.  Labor and manpower.
10. Costs and profits.
11. Standard of living (summary indicators, repairs and maintenance, housing and municipal services, domestic trade, education, cultural services, and medicine).

These targets are grouped according to section (e.g., industry, agriculture) and function (e.g., investment, labor). The latter characterizes development in individual branches as well as in the economy as a whole. At this stage of planning, initial information flows from the production targets. There are two major calculation schemes, one based on the balance of capacities, as in machine building, and the second on balance of raw materials, as in light industry and the food industry.

Despite continual attempts by Gosplan to define the concept of capacity, it remains a topic of investigation. The definition of capacity as a maximum potential output is obvious, but the problem is how to measure such output. Economic theory recommends the use of the "bottleneck" approach in which the capacity at a predetermined point is taken as the capacity of an enterprise. Finding this approach vague, some economists suggest that capacity can be measured in terms of basic equipment or particular machines and apparatus. In planning, disagreements arise in the computation of production targets because of the desires of the participants to pursue empirical paths to differing estimates of capacity. An example of the weakness of the theory is that in the coal industry actual values of output for some mines are often greater than their capacities.

Estimated capacities serve as a basis for determining potential output, which must be projected at a level close to maximum. In these calculations capacities are transformed into average annual values. Thus new capacities are divided by four and multiplied by the number of full quarters from the date of inception to the end of a year. In five-year plans, where such precise calculations are not possible, all capacities are taken to be 35 percent of annual value in the first year of installation [28]. Hence they are expected to operate approximately for the final quarter of a year. If they do not operate that long, plan targets will not be met either by those enterprises or the many others which depend on their supply. Analogous coefficients are used for capital that has undergone wear and tear.

The simplified scheme for compiling production plans in physical terms is as follows: (1) evaluation of output with existing capacities, taking into account the coefficient of their use which must be 80-90 percent; (2) evaluation of output with capacities put into use in a planned period; and (3) summary calculations.

Information concerning utilization of capacities and capital is obtained from investment plans. This is the primary link from investment to output. In turn, an investment plan depends heavily on the production of capital goods. While industrial managers complain that the construction industry continually fails to meet its plan targets, builders can place the blame on management. Another kind of link, the discrepancy between estimated demand for a commodity and actual capacity, is an indication that new investment is required. Of course it is a long time before such requirements are noted and real investments are subsequently made.

Other connections in the initial step of production plan development are formed with scientific research and technological advance planning in the national economy. In mastering the production of new commodities, enterprises first perform experimental work and then manufacture the initial industrial series. As soon as this step is completed, it is taken into consideration in corresponding production plans.

After output in physical terms has been estimated, value targets are computed in money terms. The sales revenue is determined on the basis of expected output and changes in inventories at the beginning and end of a planned period. Complications result from the need to correlate aggregate grouped prices with the industrial product mix. Another problem arises from the discrepancy between scales of measurement for physical and value indicators in planning. On the one hand, value indicators must take into account the entire output. On the other hand, the listing of production in physical terms included in the national economic plan is equal, on the average, to only 40 percent of the "broad listing" (shirokaia nomenklatura) used in planning material resource distribution. In such a situation errors and omissions are inevitable. While the 1965 Reform reduced the quantity of production in physical terms planned for enterprises, the new "Methodological Directions for the Development of National Economic Plans" approved by Gosplan in 1980 [8] require the coverage of 80-85 percent of the gross output by direct calculation in physical terms.

Once the gross value of output of industries is known, requirements for labor, wages, costs, and profits can be evaluated. Calculations based on output information start from estimates of labor productivity growth and cost reduction by factor. Such factors as technological change, improvements in management and organization of production, changes in product mix, prices, and mineral and fuel outputs, and the specificity of an industry must be considered. In the sequence of calculations, the initial number of those employed is determined first, with attention to preserving actual productivity. Then successive reductions are made for each of the above factors.

At this stage investments are allocated according to specifications (titul'nye spiski) for all large-scale consructions containing: (1) substantiation of the necessity for and appropriateness of the structure and reasons for the choice of its location; (2) verification of completed documentation, availability of construction organizations capacities and contracts for the delivery of necessary equipment; (3) information on requirements of the enterprise after completion for manpower, energy, and raw materials and on their resources; and (4) an extensive demonstration of the contribution to be made by the project.

At this time an extensive system of material balances is developed by all industrial departments for their products. It consists of aggregate balances such as electrical power, fuels, oil products, ferrous metals, nonferrous metals, chemicals and rubber technical products, construction materials, lumber, cellulose and paper products, textile and leather materials, equipment, machines and cable products, etc. In the resource part of a balance, output, imports, and changes in inventories are taken into account. The utilization part of a balance includes demands for production consumption including research and experimental work, construction, exports, and market funds for consumers, reserves, and stocks. Each balance must be supplemented by calculations of the demands of industry and construction, substantiated with approved expenditure norms. The primary condition for the latter is that they be "progressive," i.e., change from period to period in the direction of reduction. However there exists the possibility of increasing expenditures by introducing "experimental" norms for new products and technological processes.

The mutual dependence of resources and production targets is important in balancing the main indicators in national economic plans. As we saw above, resources are calculated in accordance with production targets, although in the first stage output was based on estimated limits of available resources. Now, when more precise information on demands for resources has been obtained, corrections are made in output values. Theoretically this convergence process can be seen as infinite, if a precise model is possible at all. In planning practice however there is an urgent need for empirically satisfactory results which may appear to be far from equilibrium.

An alternate system of calculation important for some extractive and consumer goods industries, unlike that described above, begins with reserves and the stock of raw materials. Capacities play an auxiliary role in this case. Since technological processes in light industry and the food industry utilize agricultural raw materials, planning calculations for these industries depend on a variety of balances for agricultural products and their distribution for further processing or domestic trade market funds. In the machine-building industry, metal availability has become a more decisive factor in many cases than production capacities.

Balances for agricultural products provide one of the most important links between agricultural and industrial indicators. They are employed by all departments responsible for the development of consumer goods production targets. The latter are the most unstable of all plan targets because of fluctuations in these same balances whose distributional parts are continually corrected. Projections for the food industry and light industry change with resource estimates. On the other hand, calculations of agricultural output depend on the information about inputs flowing from industry to agriculture. They reflect targets for delivery of fertilizer, equipment, metal, energy, etc.

If industrial calculations depend only in part on indicators resulting from the balance of the national economy (balans narodnogo khoziaistva), the character of the "nonproductive" branches of the economy is based entirely on the final product of the "productive" sphere. The state budget indicators are not used directly in planning calculations, but in aggregate form they are reflected in the balance of the national economy.

THE RELATIVE SIGNIFICANCE OF CURRENT AND PERSPECTIVE
PLANS, AND THE USE OF NORMATIVE METHODS

Official Soviet sources claim that their country
possesses a thoroughly designed system for short-,
middle-, and long-term planning.  In addition, the
Academy of Sciences develops projections for technological change and for the development of the
resource base of the economy in the future.  These
claims have found their way into Western economic
literature.  But does such a precise interlacing set of
plans operate so that plan targets follow naturally one
after another?  Or do the country and its leaders care
only about day-to-day economic problems?

In order to gain an understanding of the true
situation one must acknowledge the "directive"
character of plans.  In the 1970s, with the growing
passion for forecasting, almost everyone in economics
started to develop forecasts.  But the question to be
answered was whether there was a real need for forecasts since thousands of people were already engaged in
planning.  What was the difference, if any, between
forecasts and plans?  To some extent, all planning
calculations are predictions which must take into
account technological change, growth of the resource
base, weather conditions in agriculture, etc.  As
usual, it did not take long for "creative" writers to
find an answer.  The difference, they claimed, stemmed
from the problem of "directiveness."  Unlike plans,
forecasts lacked a directive character.  This meant
that their fulfillment by any economic unit was not
obligatory, and that they provided only preliminary
information for planners.

Analyzing the long-term (15-20 year) plan from this
standpoint, we will come to a similar conclusion about
its nonobligatory character.  As a matter of fact,

there was only one real attempt to develop such a plan, and that was for the period 1976-1990. In 1972-1973 all ministries, departments, and republics, as well as their enterprises and organizations, wrote proposals for the main guidelines for that plan. Yet little progress was made. The methodology and, we might add, the goal of this work was unclear. Scientific recommendations were made in appropriately vague terms, and planners kept to their tested approach of "planning from the bottom up." This approach was a continuation of time series with some forecasted growth rates. However there is an essential difference between imposing such rates for a coming year and extending them until 1990. For instance, what is the usefulness of this approach for agriculture in the absence of the consideration of the alternative scenarios of its organization in 1990? Indeed the growth of kolkhoz production was estimated when it is not even certain that kolkhozy will exist by that time at all.

To be effective, a plan must contain targets and limits of resources on a strict annual basis. It is obvious that the 1976-1990 long-term plan does not meet that requirement. But what about the middle-term (five-year) plans? To begin with, we must note that all post-war five-year plans before 1971 defined their targets only for the ends of the relevant periods. The 9th Five-Year Plan was the first in the history of postwar planning to determine its targets annually.

In the Soviet system plan targets are not real targets unless appropriate inputs are allocated to economic units. As mentioned in the previous chapters, enterprises and organizations are more concerned with investment, material supply, etc., because these are plan targets that must be adjusted to available resources while the reverse is not always true. Therefore it is worth mentioning that neither the 9th nor

10th five-year plans, which specified their targets on an annual basis, contained plans for the distribution of material resources among the main holders of funds, i.e., all-union ministries and departments and republic councils of ministers. All of those resources were allocated in annual plans which indicates the role and importance of these plans.

The 1979 Resolution has brought about essential changes in the distribution of resources in favor of five-year plans. The system of long-term normatives discussed below is to play the major role in that process. The 11th Five-Year Plan (1981-1985) was the first to develop plans for distribution, in this case of about 330 items of the most important materials and equipment [16]. This was a real attempt to include five-year plans in the set of mechanisms influencing the direction of national economic development.

Of special interest is the question of how the economy could function when its most valuable inputs were allocated five years in advance, leaving party and planning authorities no room to adjust the allocations. Because of this, it is most likely that necessary changes will be made using annual plans and that in the future five-year balances will not play their projected leading role in the distribution of resources.

Another reason for the relatively minor role of five-year plans has been the problem of their coordination with annual plans. Before the 9th five-year period, 1971-1975, it was impossible to compare five-year and corresponding year-by-year targets. The comparisons after 1971 demonstrated that the yearly projections made for the 9th and 10th five-year plans were higher than those for annual plans. The difference became especially pronounced with third-year targets, when five-year figures appeared to be practically useless.

The 1979 Resolution provides for considerable
changes in the temporal range of targets. Gosplan must
now develop the main guidelines for periods of ten,
rather than five years.  Targets for the first five
years are to be defined on a yearly basis, and those
for the second five years only for the end of an entire
period.  The main guidelines for five-year plans have
been changed to control figures derived from the ten-
year plan with appropriate corrections.  Substantial
changes are provided for annual plans.  There is no
longer a separate control figures stage for annual
plans since their indicators must follow directly from
five-year plans.  The most impressive provision made in
this respect is that the targets of annual plans must
not be lower than the corresponding five-year projections.  The only thing not indicated is how to
accomplish this.

We might add here that the last two claims are
contradictory.  Since the resolution does not require
the equality of targets in the two kinds of plans,
corrections must be allowed for in the transition from
five-year to annual targets.  Therefore a control
figures stage for annual plans will be needed,
regardless of what it is called, especially since it is
doubtful that five-year-plan targets will in all cases
be surpassed.

The persistent trend toward increasing the role of
five-year plans was especially evident in the unprecedented decision to dictate the limits of capital
investment only in five-year plans, without any changes
in annual plans.  This means that decisions to invest
can now be made only once in five years.  Again, as in
the case of material resources, we are skeptical on
this point.  Taking into consideration the intended
"mobilizing effect" of five-year plans, one can imagine
that they will be tough.  On the other hand, chronic

shortcomings in the construction industry and in mastery of new production processes, shortages in the supply of metal and agricultural raw materials, and the lack of resource reserves will contribute to failures in plan fulfillment. For these reasons annual changes seem inevitable.

An interesting example illustrating the scale of changes made even in annual plans can be found in an article [21] which lists the following data on the number of enterprises that failed to meet their 11- and 12-month plan targets of three recent years.

TABLE 4.1
Number of Enterprises that Did Not Meet Their Production Plan Targets (Thousands)

| Year | Estimate for 11-Month Totals | Result at the End of the Year |
|------|------------------------------|-------------------------------|
| 1977 | 4.2 | 1.9 |
| 1978 | 4.4 | 1.9 |
| 1979 | 6.6 | 2.8 |

Taking into account the existence of 43,000 production associations and enterprises in the country by the end of 1979 [16] yields that more than 15 percent of them did not meet their 11-month production targets in 1979. The writer explains the cause of dramatic improvements made by thousands of enterprises in the manufacture of commodities by the end of the year: their plan targets were reduced in December by supervising ministries and departments.

Why are planning authorities so eager to strengthen the five-year approach to plan targets even though annual targets are not met? The official explanation is that the country cannot get by, attending only to day-to-day problems, and that the implementation of long-term programs demands appropriate planning. To some extent, this is true as much as for any other nation. But there is more to it. Authorities hope that by concentrating more on five-year plans they can succeed in rationing resources on the basis of a well-designed long-term system of normatives. One of the biggest problems in this respect is the enormous investment burden on the economy.

Investment and its growth in the USSR in three recent five-year periods and in the 11th Five-Year Plan is characterized in Table 4.2 [1].* The sharp decrease in the rates of investment growth over the observed period is caused by the above-mentioned factors of production of investment capital such as construction industry capacities, supply of metal and agricultural raw materials, etc., which we will not discuss here. But the fact is that the growth of investment on the part of ministries, departments, republics, and industrial enterprises is to be reduced dramatically. Another reason for the wish to reduce the growth of new investment is the enormous number of unfinished construction projects. As explained in Chapter 2, with the normative term of building in most of the industries at about four to five years, annual investment should amount to 20-25 percent of its total estimated value. Indeed, however, annual investment is on the average several times less than that due to the correspondingly large number of previously initiated construction projects.

Each year planning authorities have been pressed by

---

*In this and in the tables 5.1 and 5.2 the plan targets are corrected according to the publications related to the 11th Five-Year Plan (Ekonomicheskaia Gazeta N48, 1981).

TABLE 4.2
Investment in the USSR by Five-Year Period (Billions of
Rubles)

| Period | Total Investment | Increase | |
|---|---|---|---|
| | | Absolute | % |
| 1966-1970 | 346 | 104 | 43 |
| 1971-1975 | 491 | 145 | 42 |
| 1976-1980 | 633 | 142 | 29 |
| 1981-1985 (plan) | 700 | 67 | 11 |

demands for more and more investment. Since many of
the demands are really well-reasoned and even urgent,
it is difficult to resist in all cases. As a consequence, new investment has been growing in spite of
the policy of strict limitation. Planning authorities
believe that the shift to a five-year term of investment allocation will improve the situation and
strengthen investment discipline. At least pressure
will be brought to bear on them only once in five yers.
Of course there is more involved in this intertemporal
consideration. Time will tell whether the system of
allocating investment funds once in five years will
work. Up to now, planning practice has given a negative answer on this question.

Increasing the role of five-year planning in
general is connected with the use of a set of long-term
normatives imposed by the 1979 Resolution. To begin
with, enterprise operations must be estimated with the
normative net value of output. As illustrated in
Chapter 2, this means that production in physical terms
is to be multiplied by the norms of net output rather
than, as in the case of gross output, by prices. The
higher the normative the lower the share of material

expenditures in total output. This approach will influence also the measurement of labor productivity as the ratio of normative net value of output to the number of employees. The transition by all ministries to planning according to the new principle of normative net value of output will come about gradually starting with the 11th five-year period, 1981-1985.

In five-year plans, the so-called "economic" normatives such as those for wages and bonus funds must also be designated. The wage normative has nothing to do with wage rates, but is merely an estimate of the proportion of wages in the total value of output. The normative is computed per ruble of output estimated, as in the planning of labor productivity, with net value of output in most cases. In the 11th Five-Year Plan, only a few ministries are to use this experimental approach [4]. The normative for the bonus fund, as we showed in Chapter 2, is defined in most cases according to labor productivity growth and the manufacture of high-quality products, with a reduction in the value of output to penalize those failing to meet plan targets for deliveries.

Further, a gradual transition to the normative principle of distribution of profits is provided starting with the 11th Five-Year Plan. At all levels of management, financial plans must be developed with annual targets. The portions of profits retained by enterprises and associations for their own needs will be determined by long-term normatives differentiated by year. Since, as in the case of the bonus fund, retained profits vary with the results of the enterprise operation, it looks as if they may grow faster with the growth of profits than was foreseen by the 1965 Reform. To some extent, the budget will be protected against this by the guaranteed values of advance payments required from the enterprises that use the normative approach to profit distribution. Funds apportioned to enterprises according to normatives depend on their needs and profitability. Yet the profitability of many industries, for example ferrous metallurgy and construction materials, is very low. For some such as coal and lumber it is negative. New wholesale prices to be introduced in 1982 are intended to improve the situation by raising prices for those industries, but not to the extent of making them self-sufficient. For this reason, experimental normatives which have already been introduced in many industries attempt to compensate for lower levels of profitability.

Thus the experimental normative in the 1979 plan for the Ministry of the Machine-Tool and Tool-Making Industry (Ministerstvo stankostroitel'noi i instrumental'noi promyshlennosti) that had a high level of profitability was 39.1, i.e., the ministry received 39.1 percent of its profit for the needs of its enterprises. For the Ministry of Agricultural Machinery (Ministerstvo traktornogo i sel'skokhoziaistvennogo mashinostroeniia) that normative was 60.1, and for the Ministries of Heavy Machinery and Power Machinery, with low levels of profitability, 73.9 and 96, respectively [33]. Such differentiations mean that relatively unprofitable industries receive greater shares of profits for exceeding their plans than do highly profitable industries with correspondingly lower normatives. Taking into consideration numerous complaints in this regard, the provision is made that in the 11th Five-Year Plan all industries will receive the same rate of 50 percent of their excess profits, or 25 percent if they surpass their plans of production by more than 3 percent.

Overlooking the arbitrariness and inflexibility of the above differentiation of normatives, we would point out one problem that cannot be solved in this way at all. Even if a fair distribution among industries were arrived at, it would have to be based on averaged estimates since each industry includes thousands of enterprises with a tremendous spectrum of profitability. No one could answer the question of how such normatives could create incentives for all of them.

Among the other resources, an extensively increasing system of norms has been developed for the expenditure of materials and equipment. Gosplan employs data on the total volume of materials used in production, and coefficients for expenditures of materials by specific goods and for each ministry as a whole. Although in setting norms for metal expenditures only 22 items are taken into account [35], very detailed norm fixing takes place for expenditures of fuel and energy. Much attention is paid to the development of norms for expenditures of metal, cement, and lumber in construction.

How are these thousands of norms and normatives being created?* The Department of Norms and Normatives (Otdel norm i normativov) of Gosplan is in charge of setting norms at the macrolevel and organizes the whole process of norm development. The Scientific Research Institute of Planning and Norms is responsible for pre-

---

*The difference between norms and normatives is not distinct in Soviet economic literature. Norms are usually set for expenditures of inputs in material production, though exceptions are possible. Estimates of the ratio of financial flows related to each other, once they are accepted officially, become normatives. Examples of this type mentioned above are the ratio of the net value of output to the gross output, wages to the net or gross value of output, the bonus fund to profit or wage bill, components of the distributiuon of profit to its total, etc.

paring cross-industry instructions which must be specified later for the various ministries by their
technological institutes. In recent years a large-
scale project for computer processing of normatives
(avtomatizirovannaia sistema normativov) has been initiated. Despite large amounts of labor and money
contributed, the project has proved relatively unpro-
ductive. As there is little interesting research to be
done in this type of data processing, it is difficult
to enlist skilled specialists. What is most damaging
is that the institutes conducting the work are isolated
from the production processes. Because of this Gosplan
and the ministries still use their own approach to
norm fixing on the basis of actual expenditures in the
past (po baze), with corrections for increases in efficiency. In such a situation this may be the only
reasonable policy. The problem is that those for whom
the norms are set, aware of this principle, take care
that the norms are not "too taut."

As discussed above, by increasing the role of long-
term normatives planning authorities expect to decrease
yearly demands for resources. What's more, such developments represent a trend in the direction of further
centralization of decision making in planning. With
the expansion of normative data in Gosplan, which
doubled between the 9th and 10th five-year plan periods
[35], Gosplan will depend less on data from ministries
and will increase its control of them.

Surprisingly enough, the ministries and their
enterprises are also interested in the development of
normatives. Two major factors are responsible for
this. First, the availability of norms and normatives
helps them to substantiate their demands for resources.
Second, in the normative approach profits, financial
funds, and, what is more important for enterprises,

wages and bonuses are bound to the results of their operations. Thus by increasing output, enterprises can receive higher wage funds, in contrast to the situation with inflexible wage limits. With further development of the new approach of course more constraints and regulations will be imposed to manage the process of wage growth.

MATERIAL BALANCES IN PLANNING AND THE USE OF INPUT-OUTPUT TABLES

The use of material balances in Soviet planning has been thoroughly investigated in the West (see, for example, [23] or [6]). The usual focus is on their role as planning instruments in the material supply system. Their role however is more important than that. The major task of the material supply system in planning is plan development for the distribution of materials and equipment based on corresponding balances. Most of the balances are worked out in the elaborating of production plans, with much broader purposes than those for the supply system.

Each industrial department of Gosplan responsible for planning the output of a line of products must collect information from other industries which manufacture any of the same products, and also must know about demands from other departments for these products. In such a procedure, the output of and demands for goods and services are mutually adjusted. The two main demands -- for production use and for market funds for the consumers -- are evaluated differently. The former is computed on the basis of expenditure norms per unit of output and draft projections for output of goods. Computation of the latter is based on distribution data for market funds in the previous year, these being revised according to current information.

Thus material balances have a great effect on the

output plans in many industries. For example, the electrical power, coal, oil, gas, metal, and other production plans cannot be compiled without balancing the inputs with "satisfied" ministry and department demands for them (as explained above, "satisfied" demand is determined on the basis of supply projections and is usually lower than what the users ask for). The ministries using these inputs must adapt their production targets to changes in supply. This is possible because all Gosplan departments, either producing or demanding a specific product, operate with the same norms for expenditure of inputs per unit of output, which transform corrections in projected supply into corrections in final output. Possessing confirmed norms for expenditures of its products per unit of output for all industries, each department performs calculations for product demands both total and specialized. Personal and public consumption norms exist or are being developed for many products, and these norms are employed in analogous calculations. Consequently there are repeated mutual verification and control over the work of different departments.

Links similar to those between production plans exist also between production and investment plans. Material balances indicate the material, energy, and equipment supply limits for new construction in all industries. Relevant "satisfied" demand changes lead to fluctuations in construction industry capacities as well as in the output levels of affected industries. There exists also another type of relation between production and construction plans. When a discrepancy arises between production capacity and product demand which, according to priorities, must be satisfied, then feedback from a material balance signals the necessity for new construction or expansion of the existing capacity.

Material balances are important also in establishing the above relations between agriculture and consumer goods industries. Prior to the calculation of balances for agricultural products used in the production of consumer goods, accurate projections for the latter are impossible. Domestic trade is in a similar situation both with respect to balances of agricultural products and of consumer goods. These balances form the basis for preparing distribution plans for materials and equipment and, further, delivery plans. Thus they provide links also between transportation and all other branches of the economy.

Some Western analysts and Soviet economists in academic circles underestimate the regulating role of material balances and link them only with the supply system. Planners however take great pride in the balance method and consider it one of the greatest achievements of planning theory and practice. We have doubts about the theory since there is nothing new in this approach. For practical purposes however the planners have indeed organized the system of balances so that they do make a positive contribution to the planning process.

For the 1981-1985 Five-Year Plan, Gosplan had to prepare some 400 material balances and distribution plans for more than 80 percent of its products [8]. For the 1981 annual plan, there were more than 2,000 balances. In contrast, the number of balances being developed by republic gosplans was much less than 100, reflecting the extent of centralization in the allocation of resources. As centralization increases, the number of balances has increased dramatically.

Two Gosplan departments organize the whole process of elaborating material balances -- the Summary Department of Material Balances and Plans for Distribution of Materials (Otdel material'nykh balansov i planov ras-

predeleniia) and the Summary Department of Equipment
Balances and Plans for Distribution of Equipment (Otdel
balansov i planov raspredeleniia oborudovaniia). As
mentioned above, most of the balances are developed by
the industrial departments in Gosplan. The task of
these two summary departments is to coordinate the work
done on balances and to develop those balances that are
not the responsibility of any particular industrial
department. In addition, these two summary departments
collect information about the fulfillment of delivery
plans, and draw up material resource distribution plans
for the use of the main holders of the related funds
(fondoderzhateli).

In connection with production plans, we noted above
the problem of coordinating the "broad" and "narrow"
categories (nomenklatura) of commodities. The latter,
covering some 40 percent of all manufactured goods, is
used to evaluate production plans in physical terms,
while the estimate of the former is used to plan the
gross value of output. The allocation plans for
material resources are based evidently on the broad
category, which is not yet known in the planning process. Thus much confusion often arises further along
in the process, especially when plan specifications are
compiled, and so numerous deviations from the desired
projections are inevitable. As a consequence of
replacing required materials with whatever is available, input amounts and costs increase and product
quality decreases.

The discrepancy between planned and allocated
resources exists not only for material inputs, but also
for consumer goods. In a national economic plan,
domestic trade sales (tovarooborot) are determined in
money terms and then are itemized based on the broad
category balance. In other words, in planning domestic
trade commodities flowing to consumers are not speci-

fied precisely until allocation plans for material inputs are developed.

The above examples show that allocation plans for material inputs reflect the results of enterprise operations better than production plans. The role of allocation funds has been growing in recent years since the deliveries indicator has begun to affect incentive funds. Now far more attention is paid to the methodological problems of developing material balances and computerizing their calculations. We will mention here two such methodological problems.

The first problem is related to the commensurability of indicators in material balances. Although the indicators are developed in physical terms, they must be aggregated. For example, even a monoproduct such as coal is an aggregate. The Council of Ministers approves the balances and allocation plans for coal resources as a whole, designating also the coal of particular areas such as the Kuznetsk and Donetsk Basins, and then Gosplan specifies the coal by grade and quality. Improving the measurement of material balances is a constant problem at Gosplan research institutes. Units in use such as metric tons, meters, square meters, etc., do not reflect product utility. Standardized measures such as calories, units of capacity and power, contents of a pure substance, etc., sometimes apply, but often the meaning of aggregate balances is arbitrary. Probably the most important instance of such shortcomings is in the case of rolled metal balances, which have been discussed in planning for many years.

The second of the methodological problems noted above involves the interdependence of material balances. The problem here lies in substitution among material inputs and in the fact that a product noted once as output serves many times as input. Therefore a change in one of the balances has to be transferred to many others, and this chain of corrections can affect a large number of industries and administrative units. Gosplan can handle this problem in two ways. One is by developing aggregate balances for mutually substituted resources (among them, the consolidated balance of fuels and energy proved to be especially helpful in planning). The second is by developing input-ouput tables.

The ex-post input-output tables for 1959, 1966, and 1972 were compiled by the Central Statistics Administration (TsSU) and its scientific institute. They were published in part and, in reconstructed form, are widely used by Western analysts (an authoritative source is the monograph [50]). Our interest is in the use of input-output tables in planning. At two of the Gosplan research organizations -- the Scientific Research Economic Institute (Nauchno-issledovatel'skii ekonomicheskii institut) and the Main Computer Center (Glavnyi vychislitel'nyi tsentr) -- there are special departments which are responsible for developing the methodology, instructions, computer programs, and data base for input-output tables.

Several models were created to bring these tables closer to the Gosplan classification of industries, products, and output requirements. Included was a model for 18 branches of the economy as well as for the main aggregated branches of industry, and also a model containing the gross output in physical terms of some 260 products [19]. One of the Main Computer Center's models incorporated input-output tables and attempted to minimize target deviations between annual and five-year plans [52].

Calculations based on these models have been performed by the above institutes yearly and submitted to Gosplan. Participation by Gosplan departments in such

work is minimal and limited usually to the analysis of
the final results. In 1972-1973, during the preparation of guideline proposals for the 15-year plan, there
was an attempt to involve the major planning institutions in the development of input-output tables. All
ministries had to furnish information on technological
coefficients of material and energy expenditures by all
other ministries per unit of output. The ministries'
scientific and technological institutes were charged
with computing these coefficients. However, from
Gosplan's standpoint, the project was largely a failure
[53]. Some reasons in brief are the following.

Although input-output coefficients are called technological, they reflect the state of technology only if
the models are very detailed. At a high level of
aggregation, these coefficients express for each
industry the vector of ratios of its inputs by
industrial origin to its gross value of output. Branch
institutes performed the sequence of calculations as
follows: (1) verification of projected or desired plan
targets for the ministries; (2) computation of
corresponding input flows as requested by the
ministries, and (3) division of the latter by the
former. However, if ministry projections did not
satisfy Gosplan or changes in plan targets were inevitable for other reasons, then the coefficients could
not be used. The sequence of calculations would have
to be repeated again and again, a process considered
too costly for the promised gains.

It is not necessary at this point to discuss the
disadvantages of input-output tables. Nor do we need
to reexamine the assertion that planners are too conservative to accept advanced techniques. We think that
two successive stages -- illusion and disillusion --
have been typical when employing mathematical methods
in Soviet economics. Those who try to introduce these

methods are to some extent responsible for this. Exaggerating the possibilities of mathematical methods, they confidently apply conclusions from model simulations directly to real economic situations. After the creation of such a new "remedy," a campaign for its use begins. If successful, then the decision to begin an experiment in Gosplan is made by its chairman. All or some of the departments must assist the research institute running the experiment in collecting information and analyzing results. But once the planners familiarize themselves with the suggested techniques, they begin to see the discrepancy between promised and actual results.

Let us examine this in the case of input-output. First, input-output tables cannot replace material balances, as some Soviet economists have suggested. The major principle of a balance lies in the double-entry accounting of resources and outlays. It is advantageous to have two different sources of information for assets and liabilities, so that some specified items can be used in balancing. The input-output procedure suggests one-sided computation of industrial gross outputs beginning with final demands for the various products. Thus although the idea itself is fruitful, planners find great difficulties in applying this model directly to balancing material resources and their allocations. The aggregating problem in input-output analysis also creates difficulties when different levels of output are considered.

Second, as noted above, planners use material balances to coordinate production capacities with production plans, as well as to coordinate the latter with investment plans, output indicators in physical and money terms, etc. When they find in the input-output model that some of the above indicators must be fixed exogenously in order to find the relevant counterparts endogenously, they are disappointed.

For other reasons also, planners discover that the input-output model is not very useful to them. For example, the planners think that determining final demand components is even more difficult than determining gross output. Indeed the Soviet economy is oriented on a sequence of calculations opposite to that for free-market economies. Since the demand for goods and services in the Soviet economy is substituted with "satisfied" demand, which is derived from the level of output, planners believe they can determine production plans more precisely than they can components of final demand.

While the attitude of Gosplan specialists toward input-output is not favorable, there have been changes in the field due to increased computerization of planning calculations. Input-output tables are suggested for use at the macrolevel of the economy at all steps of this large-scale project. It is really difficult to imagine computerized planning calculations without input-output tables.

Finally, we will add the following. Although, as mentioned above, input-output tables were sugested for use in problems for which they were not suitable, their real possibilities for planning have never been discovered. They were employed in forecasting models, not in economic analysis which is far more important for Gosplan. As a matter of fact, the Soviet ex-post input-output tables have been used, for the purpose of analyzing the Soviet economy, more in the United States than in the Soviet Union. There is no doudbt that the unique information provided by these tables could be very helpful to Soviet planners were they developed regularly. For example, the analysis of the full input coefficients and expenditures could be fruitful in many fields, especially in evaluating the efficiency of different industries.

## COMPUTERIZATION OF PLANNING CALCULATIONS

Along with the more frequent employment of the normative approach and the greater role of material balances, the increased use of computers is one of the major developments in planning since the loss of faith in the 1965 Reform. It began in the late 1960s with the creation of Gosplan's Subdepartment of the Organization of the Automated Planning Calculations System (Podotdel organizatsii avtomatizirovannoi sistemy planovykh raschetov -- ASPR). Since the early 1970s this project has expanded at an unprecedented rate. Lists of organizations that have contributed to it are dozens of pages in length.

Planning technology is undoubtedly backward. Thousands of calculations are performed manually, and locating sources of information demands much time and effort. The standard attitude blaming failures of the economy on shortcomings in planning, coupled with propaganda about the wonders of programming, created a feeling that much could be done to improve planning by introducing advanced techniques. While not naive on this point, planning authorities do consider this development positive. First, even if the vast improvements promised by scientific institutes do not occur, planning authorities expect that some data banks will be established and some informational flows will be processed with computers. Second, by encouraging the development of ASPR, planning authorities demonstrate their willingness to improve the planning process. At the same time, the ASPR project does not create new problems for planners since their involvement is minimal.

Since Gosplan is a union-republic institution, ASPR
is set up at both the union and republic levels. Addi-
tionally, automated control systems (avtomatizirovannye
sistemy upravleniia -- ASU's) are developed for ministries and departments, territorial units such as economic regions, administrative regions, and cities, and
industrial territorial complexes. Under highly centralized planning and allocation of resources, the
interaction between ASPR and ASU's of the ministries
and departments is most important. Besides industrial
ASU's, there are the following specialized systems for
state committees and departments: The Automated State
Statistics System (ASGS); the Automated System for
Processing Data for Prices (ASOITsen) and the Automated
System for Financial Calculations (ASFR); ASU for the
Development of Science and Technology (ASUNT) and ASU's
for the State Committee for Construction, the State
Committee for Material and Technical Supply, the State
Committee of Standards, the State Bank, and the
Construction Bank.

Within Gosplan, ASPR incorporates more than fifty
subsystems divided into three levels: (1) the summary
national economic plan; (2) the summary resource and
balance systems; and (3) industrial and other branch
subsystems. Among second-level subsystems are those
such as Development of Science and Technology, Capital
Investment, Labor and Manpower, Costs and Profits,
Standard of Living, Territorial Planning and Allocation
of Productive Forces, Foreign Economic Relations,
Balances and Plans for Inputs Allocation, etc. [7].

The development of ASPR has three general phases of
project documentation: (1) draft; (2) technical; and
(3) working. The draft project documentation was
created for the system as a whole and contains special
volumes which describe requirements for the methods of
calculation, problems of information supply, software

specifications, computers and technical sources, and organization of work. The technical and working phases must describe schemes for solving planning problems, simulation models and methods, data bases, program packages, etc.

To circumvent the problem of meeting deadlines for completed portions of the project, its creators found it convenient to make alterations in their work for as long as funds were available. According to their explanation, the above-described documentation addresses only the problems of the "first list" (zadachi pervoi ocheredi). The number of lists to come is not established. There are no set time limits for solving problems and, while the "first list" of planning problems is often developed in detail, much of the project is outlined in vague form. The development of project documentation thus becomes a repeatable process.

From the beginning, ASPR was declared to be a powerful means for improving planning. Most planning calculations were to be replaced with the methods of optimal programming or, in Russian terminology, "optimal planning." Gradually however planners have adopted a more realistic attitude toward optimal planning, even though the official position on ASPR has not changed. Evidence of this new attitude is provided in a 1978 article [15] by the head of the Subdepartment of the ASPR Organization.

The author writes that, in annual planning, the problems of direct data processing are of primary concern. Direct planning calculations amount to 90 percent of the whole workload. More sophisticated models are used for five-year and long-term planning, due to the complicated character of perspective plans and the greater role played by preliminary stages when different alternatives are investigated. Thus 35 and 43

percent of the calculations in five-year and long-term
planning, respectively, should be handled on the basis
of optimal programming. The preciseness of these
estimates, even if doubtful, does not matter. Important here is the admission that in ASPR most calculations for annual plans will merely be replaced by data
processing. Owing to this, classification systems for
manufactured goods, for industries, enterprises, and
organizations, assorted production processes, etc.,
have been completed. A standard classification for
technical and economic terms and indicators used in
planning has been under development for many years,
however it is still not completed.

Another important development in connection with
ASPR is the centralization of control over plan
fulfillment. Such control had previously been left to
the ministries, but during the 9th and 10th five-year
plans Gosplan's role here increased. Taking into
account the tremendous amount of information necesary
to exercise such control, planning authorities expect
ASPR to develop the appropriate data base and data processing technology. Along with the stages of planning
such as control figures, draft plans, and assignments
of targets, ASPR also includes the control stage for
all types of plans and all their indicators. The
control functions include analysis of accounting data,
forecasting results of enterprise operations and
deviations from the plan, investigation of factors
causing the deviations, and suggestions for ways to
meet plan targets.

Information for the control stage is provided in
part by ministries, departments, and enterprises. It
is worth noting here that when the ASPR concept was
being developed, there were two different approaches to
it. According to one, Gosplan was to be restricted
only to information provided by ministries and depart-

ments. This approach was rejected in favor of one in which Gosplan would process information coming directly from enterprises in order to increase the reliability of computations.

The explanation of the development pattern taken by ASPR is clear: ASPR cannot deviate from actual planning practice and its emphasis on centralization of decision making, verification of calculations, and control of decisions made at ministry level. Indeed there is not much room for changes in planning techniques through ASPR, even if its developers possessed the required skills. ASPR must follow the existing planning methodology, and elaborate only such alterations as are approved by Gosplan. Otherwise the suggested techinques could not be applied, and Gosplan would not pay for them. For example, to be useful for Gosplan, the Subsystem of Balances and Plans for Inputs Allocation must include all the features of the allocation system even though the latter is highly criticized by some economists. If such an allocation were replaced with some type of market mechanism, the corresponding part of ASPR would have to be discarded.

As a matter of fact, calculation technology in ASPR is based on existing planning technology. Therefore the following question arises. Why conduct a large-scale project through numerous research institutes if the best they can do is to repeat this technology? It is necessary however to know the planning system to realize that such a question cannot be raised there. An important factor is also that planning institutions do not include in their staffs computer programmers and analysts, who are concentrated in research institutes. Without going into further detail, we will note only that Gosplan is not the place for experiments; these must be undertaken by its institutes.

In working on ASPR, each institute spends tremendous amounts of time studying and describing planning technology. This work has resulted in many volumes of documentation. The creators of this documentation have developed it mostly for their own use, and since the documentation describes the work's intermediate results it is part of ongoing research. In 1976-1978 I reviewed some of the project documentation for industrial subsystems in order to develop a "typical" (tipovoi) project for a model acceptable at this level of planning. The quality of what I read was very poor, and the corresponding parts of the technical project for ASPR were not even prepared for computer programming. It was difficult to ascertain the purpose of these materials.

Another shortcoming of the project, a result of planners not taking part in it, concerns the problem of coordinating different parts of the system. Developing plan targets, planners use their own experience and personal contacts in coordinating many details of their work. Gradually they find consistent answers to many questions. Experience and contacts however are not formalized. With people working in different fields and on different parts of the system, the development of a formalized approach is required. This is very difficult to do; it is a crucial problem for ASPR.

As was admitted by Gosplan Deputy Chairman Lebedinskii, who is the head of the Gosplan Main Computer Center and the chief designer of ASPR, the design process for the "first list" of problems suffered from serious shortcomings [22]. The problems were solved in a separate regime and not coordinated within or among the subsystems. There was a lack of methodological, informational, and organizational compatibility of different instructions and methods. No data base for ASPR was created. Information circulating among subsystems did not flow directly from one computer to another, i.e., some manual processing was still required.

Of course much of this was not difficult to foresee. At a 1973 conference, for example, I had suggested that, before beginning the large-scale project, a macro subsystem, "Main Indicators of the National Economic Plan," should be created first. It would incorporate indicators flowing from all parts of the system. Once the subsystem began operation, other work could begin on the basis of the methodology derived from it. Otherwise it would be difficult to know in what direction everyone should work. One of the leading designers of ASPR sharply replied that all necesarry subsystems were provided and there was no need for "inventions."

Nevertheless seven years later, in 1980, such a subsystem, under the name "Central Planning Calculations Complex," was officially initiated [18]. It incorporates the following groups of calculations: (1) industry demands for material, labor, and financial resources; (2) balances of the most important products, investment goods, fixed capital, productive capacities, and manpower; (3) production plans in physical and money terms by industry and ministry; (4) variants for the development and location of industries and production associations; (5) domestic trade supply with commodities in physical terms; (6) exports and imports of goods and services; and (7) some other indicators for the balance of the national economy. The number of problems handled by the subsystem will grow, and so will its influence on all calculations in ASPR. Since problems in different parts of ASPR had been solved separately, the designers decided that these sections would have to be revised and defined adequately for insertion in the above subsystem. This means that the process of formulating and solving the problems must start over from scratch.

As mentioned above, planning authorities know that millions of bits of planning information must be processed by computers. From this standpoint they consider the ASPR project useful. Yet hundreds of organizations take part in developing ASPR, making it a typical example of a highly ineffective large-scale Soviet project.

METHODOLOGICAL CHANGES AND ECONOMIC METHODS OF MANAGEMENT

We have classified all significant changes in planning in the recent fifteen-year period in three categories -- economic, organizational, and methodological. Obviously methodological as well as organizational improvements can be consistent with the command principle in planning and management. The relative roles of the three categories have changed over time in relation to the strengthening of the command principle.

The 1965 Reform resulted in the significant reorganization of the economy and in centralization of decision making and allocation of resources. The mixed branch and territorial economic structures were replaced with the direct vertical principle of management for most production enterprises. These organizational changes were accompanied by attempts to introduce some limited economic management methods at the enterprise level. These attempts were not successful. There were many reasons for the lack of success in this area, and in our opinion the conservative attitude of the planning authorities was not the most important. As explained in Chapter 2, enterprises were not prepared to make use of greater economic opportunities due mainly to the complete absence of responsibility for utilized resources.

With the failure of attempts to increase labor productivity and to meet the nation's economic needs, the role of methodological improvements has grown a great deal. The strengthening of both discipline and the command principle required an adequate methodology. The main methodological changes involved reassessment of the relative importance of five-year and annual plans, the increased use of material balances and norms in planning all economic indicators, introduction of economic normatives in the distribution of wages, profits, and incentive funds, the changes in evaluating operations, and the attempts to computerize planning calculations.

It is widely believed that, if the planning methodology is improved, the Soviet economy will perform better. Such a belief stems from erronerously blaming failures in the Soviet economy on shortcomings in plans themselves. Of course Western analysts are not so naive that they accept this explicitly. But accustomed to a free-market economy in which Adam Smith's "invisible hand" still operates in the face of various problems, Western analysts think in terms of decision makers and believe that much in the economy depends on making the right decisions. Moreover the assumption is made that in a planned economy the central authorities are all powerful. They possess control over national resources and can direct the latter in the best interests of the nation, not having to worry about the popularity of their decisions. This is true with respect to the question of control and to some extent popularity, but not so concerning power.

In an economy in which economic fundamentals do not work, the effects of a right decision do not differ essentially from those of a wrong one. One must emphasize the fact that forces other than the decisions of planners determine the economy's performance. Further, the concepts of right and wrong are arbitrary in general and depend heavily on the assumption of rationality. This concept however is too vague when applied to a planned economy. If planners' decisions are rational within their constraints, are the constraints rational as well? Or if planners put their best efforts into the material supply system, is this system justified? Our answer to this latter question under existing conditions is yes. Eliminating this supply system would only result in increased theft in the economy as a whole. This of course does not mean that the supply system itself will contribute to economic efficiency. Thus we see that a decision can be right from one standpoint and wrong from another.

It is obvious that the Soviet leaders do not want to make fundamental changes in the economy. They provided a general restructuring of the system in 1965 and staked new hopes on a reform that proved unsuccessful. We doubt they would initiate another reform of such magnitude, particularly since the options are limited if extreme changes are to be avoided. Obviously a new reform might require a move in the direction opposite to that pursued by the present leaders. Under such conditions planners can do little more than try to fill gaps in methodology.

To a certain extent, the importance of methodological improvements has been exaggerated also by Soviet economic literature. The writers know what is open to discussion and what is taboo. The topic of introducing economic management methods was addressable only in the first years of the 1965 Reform. In describing the methodological problems of planning which do not touch upon the principles of the economic system, there is more freedom. Nonetheless these are classified in two ways: open to comment in the press, or restricted to the secret channels and special memos submitted to the Central Committee and republic communist party organs.

The topics open for discussion are always regulated, though attitudes may change over time. For example, economic literature in the 1970s was full of articles describing the advantages and disadvantages of the net value of output and its normative version. Yet once the Central Committee adopted the 1979 Resolution that declared the transition to the evaluation of enterprise operations with this indicator, the dispute ceased. Since then, at least by official definition, the normative net value of output has no shortcomings. Of course the official position on this could change in the future.

Economic censors regularly receive lists of topics forbidden for discussion. For example, I was once told by a censor that, for a stipulated period of time, I was not to publish the results of macroeconomic forecasts. The reason was that the main guidelines for the 1976-1980 Five-Year Plan were under consideration, and related comments were taboo until the guidelines were approved. The permission was later given but with two reservations. First, forecasts were to be made only until 1980, i.e., not beyond those provided by the planning and party authorities. Second, the forecasts must not contradict the figures of the adopted guidelines.

It is considered a privilege to write a memo to the Central Committee. Most often these memos are the result of special assignments given to institutes by the Central Committee, Gosplan, or other authorities. The memos are concerned with the fulfillment of numerous resolutions or special inspections at enterprises. Sometimes a hypothetical research project is judged quite important by the heads of an institute, and they may ask for permission to write a memo concerning it to the Central Committee. Poor conditions in a specific industry or in the economy as a whole are discussed more openly in these memos than they would be in the press.

The introduction of methodological innovations takes the form of campaigns. Most of those initiated by scholars come from the West. In such cases a partial solution for a minor problem can grow to the scale of a remedy for the whole economy, often due to the efforts of dishonest or unqualified but energetic figures. In such a way, for example, a resolution by the Council of Ministers on the introduction of network planning (known in the West as PERT) appeared in 1966 [39]. All ministries and departments were then obligated to use network models in planning and running large projects. Starting in 1968, the planning and financing of new construction had to be done on the basis of this new method.

One of the projects of my team at that time was connected with the introduction of network planning in Ukrainian Gosplan. We created a graph describing the development of the national economic plan which included more than 5,000 operations together with their complete characteristics. We reported to the Ukrainian Gosplan's Summary Department of the National Economic Plan (Svodnyi otdel narodnokhoziaistvennogo plana) on the progress in planning operations. Actually the process gradually fell behind the schedule for the network, which soon lost its value. Although I received a document confirming the introduction of the network model and the success of the experiment, Ukrainian Gosplan has not used network planning again. Network planning failed in construction work too, as could be expected. Network schedules were not what builders needed; they needed a more reliable flow of supply. There were a few successful experiments but only in cases of special construction projects (e.g., stroiki TsK or komsomol'skie stroiki), which had a high priority for material and equipment supply. In the end, the above resolution was completely forgotten. This was just one example of the innovations which economic science has offered in planning and management. In our view, the role of economic science in economic planning and decision making has been insignificant. There are many reasons for this, but we would like only to note at this point that while scientists usually are viewed as progressive and planners as conservative, the real situation is not quite so well-defined. Scientific institutes conduct their research in isolation from work done in planning. These institutes need the opportunity to experiment, but no such possibility exists in planning. Access to planning information is very limited for them. One exception is the Main Computer Center (GVTs), which has the privilege of being a Gosplan department. On the other hand, none of the four Gosplan research institutes -- Scientific Research Economic Institute (Nauchno-issledovatel'skii ekonomicheskii institut), Scientific Research Institute of Planning and Norms (Nauchno-issledovatel'skii institut planirovaniia i normativov), Council for Studies on Production Forces (Sovet po izucheniiu proizvoditel'nykh sil), and Institute of Complex Transportation Problems (Institut kompleksnykh transportnykh problem) -- not to mention academic institutes, has privileged access to Gosplan information. For these and many other reasons, planning research results are often inadequate. One example of this is the so-called system for the optimally functioning economy suggested in [11]. After much heated controversy about this system, little emerged other than confusion over how optimal programming could be applied to the entire economy.

From our experience with planners we can say that they are skeptical about the application of econo-

132

metric, optimal programming or any other mathematical technique. We might add that the situation is the same in many other countries. But in the Soviet Union there is good reason for skepticism. Thousands of experienced people are involved in planning calculations, with mutual control and coordination at numerous intermediate steps. For this reason methodological improvement derived from optimal programming techniques does not seem too helpful for them. These people know how to substantitate plan targets. What they do not know is what to do so that the optimal plan will work. Yet this problem is beyond pure methodological considerations and lies at the heart of the economic system. Up to now, as we illustrated, the attempts to introduce limited economic methods of management have failed. The attitude of planners to these economic methods is mixed. On the one hand, many clearly understand that some changes in principle need to be made. On the other hand, they are reluctant to accept measures involving major changes.

# 5
# Conclusions

## THE ROLE OF PLANNING RESOLUTIONS AND THE WEB OF INCONSISTENCIES

The present discussion covers a fifteen-year period in which numerous resolutions and decrees on planning were adopted. These were concentrated on the planning system as a whole, on its divisions such as branches and regions, and on specific problems. In this respect, activity in this period was rather intense. It was encouraged by Gosplan through special newly appointed interdepartmental commissions (mezhduvedom-stvennye komissii) and the Department for the Introduction of New Methods of Planning and Economic Stimulation (Otdel po vnedreniiu novykh metodov plani-rovaniia i ekonomicheskogo stimulirovaniia).

As mentioned above, the 1965 resolutions undertook overall organizational as well as some methodological changes in the economy. The 1973 Resolution declared restructuring of the middle level of management to bring the centralization principle closer to the level of material production. The 1979 Resolution provided major methodological changes in planning to make it consistent with the command principle in the economy. Besides these, many other less general resolutions illuminate the situation and the workings of the planning system.

133

It is known that the adoption of a resolution signals a bad situation. Moreover, the same problem may be discussed repeatedly within a short period of time. This means not only that the previous resolutions failed but also that the problem is too important to be abandoned. For example, on the average one resolution per year adopted during the fifteen-year period in question called for improvement of consumer services and domestic trade and the manufacture of more and better-quality consumer goods. We will not discuss the fates of these resolutions which are known. More important here is that a resolution, as the culmination of the planning procedure, is affected by the same problems as the latter.

The mobilizing effect of planning is important for an understanding of these resolutions. Each ministry or department touched by a resolution must do its best to comply with it or at least to create such an appearance, whether or not the requirements of the resolution can in fact be met. To a large extent, each resolution introduces some incentive in the form of additional wages, bonuses, staff, investment, etc. However, for the leaders of the ministries and departments, the problem of their personal responsibility is more pressing. If things are going badly, the ministries or departments involved are always found guilty. Otherwise everyone and, consequently, the system would be seen as guilty. In this way each additional resolution addressed to a specific economic body transforms the constant threat of punishment from implicit to explicit. That is why party and planning authorities find the resolutions helpful in maintaining some level of discipline in the bureaucratic hierarchy.

As discussed in preceding chapters, the mobilizing effect is considered fruitful in planning even when plan targets are not met. The resolutions in question are intended to play the same stimulating role for specified industries and for the planning system as a whole. In other words, everyone becomes used to the idea that resolutions are not complied with. What is important is the degree of such noncompliance. Here again, as in planning in general, priorities begin to work.

Each of the resolutions is concerned with the improvements in a specific direction or branch of the economy. Resolutions concerning agriculture of course outnumber by far those in other areas. Nevertheless much attention was paid to the development of construction, ferrous metallurgy, machine building, etc., not to mention classified resolutions related to the development of the industries producing military hardware. The major problem for all resolutions is that the improvements they call for require the utilization of additional inputs which, in turn, is possible only through the reallocation of resources throughout the economy.

Since inputs are scarce and there are so many resolutions, resolutions themselves must have different priorities with respect to inputs allocation. As discussed earlier, these priorities range from industries working for the military complex to industries producing the means of production, including those serving agriculture. Then follow industries manufacturing consumer goods and, last, consumer services. Again, these priorities are materialized in national economic plans because the ministries whose industries drew special attention have to adjust their plan targets to new goals imposed by relevant resolutions.

Although resolutions cannot change completely the direction of inputs allocation, they do influence planners' priorities within whatever

limited leeway the planners may have. Yet their impact
can be only temporary since with time other resolutions
are adopted, and older ones lose their importance.
Natural forces of the economy begin to reduce the
effect of temporary improvements and reveal close relationships among different aspects of economic development and growth. Official attitude toward those
resolutions is nevertheless positive since they play
the role of injections into economic activity.

For example, several resolutions adopted by the
Council of Ministers and Gosplan on the introduction of
mathematical methods and computers into planning proved
essential to the operation of scientific institutes and
computer centers which, as a result of these resolutions, were able to get funding for research. In
dealing with planners the institutes were able to quote
the resolutions on the importance of mathematical
methods. In 1969 the Central Committee and the Council
of Ministers adopted the Resolution on the Use of
Mathematical Methods and Computers in Agricultural
Planning, Accounting, and Management. Agriculture did
not increase its production, but the huge Institute of
Cybernetics in Agriculture was created providing many
scholars with good jobs. Every cloud has a silver
lining.

Regardless of the body adopting a resolution or
related document -- Gosplan, Council of Ministers,
Supreme Soviet, Central Committee -- they are all prepared by Gosplan departments. Preparing resolutions and
all types of information for the leaders at all levels,
including their speeches, is a significant function of
planners. When these assignments are considered of
great importance, scientists are invited to take part.
Their role is often limited to taking part in conferences and discussions, which seems to satisfy all
involved.

The main issues in all of these resolutions --
productivity and efficiency -- are directly related to
the problems of centralization, decentralization,
incentives, and responsibility discussed in the previous chapters. The advocates of the 1965 Reform
viewed the decentralization of the Soviet economy as a
process of transferring economic decision making from
the top level of management to the enterprises, where
material production takes place and it is easier to
make efficient decisions. Such a view, which is
widespread, seems inappropriate for the Soviet economy,
as it does not take into consideration the absence of
economic responsibility on the part of enterprise managers.

A unit is said to have economic responsibility only
if payments for inputs come from the pockets of its
owners or equivalent parties. The 1965 Reform
attempted to develop incentives which could stimulate
the economy to move only in the direction of utilizing
more and more resources, without providing any real
possibility for balancing managers' targets -- higher
wages and bonuses -- with their economic responsibility. What the economy needs is a system of "counter-
incentives," i.e., incentives not to use resources when
the opportunity cost is too high. Private ownership,
with the risk of loss and bankruptcy, may not always be
socially attractive but does serve a purpose. As a
matter of fact, no economic theory can create the image
that you pay from your own pocket if you do not.

A common objection to market economies is that most
of their industrial firms are depersonalized, and their
managers do not share in economic responsibility.
Without going into a general discussion, a brief
example will point up the distinction between the two
systems. High interest rates, which dissuade the
Western entrepreneur from investing, would be insignif-

icant for a Soviet enterprise since its expenditures are covered in any event. The only problem could be getting investment funds from planning authorities.

Observing the operation of the planning system, I came gradually to realize that it had developed a system of administrative and regulatory measures to protect the economy from the lack of economic responsibility of its parts. Of course these measures have worked as barriers and have not stimulated the economy. Planners are usually blamed for poor economic performance, but without their contributions the situation would probably be even worse.

In our opinion, the fundamental principle of these protective measures is the separation of the decision-making process from the possibility of personal gain. It has nothing to do with the managerial incentive system which works rather in the opposite direction. Centralization is a logical outgrowth of this principle since it increases the distance between enterprises, where decisions can be turned into material gains, and the decision makers. Thus managers of enterprises do not have much opportunity to regulate their own bonuses, and those making decisions at the top level of management are not rewarded directly by their decisions. Duplication of functions, mutual control, starting calculations from scratch at all levels, a strict normative approach to the allocation of resources, etc., are among the measures helpful in pursuing the above principle. Doubtless the economy cannot perform effectively under such conditions. On the other hand, when nobody has economic responsibility and national resources are free, stealing is a greater evil and one which can destroy the economy completely.

By stealing we understand here different possibilities to benefit at society's expense rather than direct stealing of commodities from enterprises and organizations. At a plenum of the Central Committee held in the mid-1970s, Brezhnev said that the economy loses 25 billion rubles annually due to theft of goods, and another 25 billion due to speculation by individuals. We know how unreliable estimates used in planning can be if they are not based on accounting data, especially estimates of this sort, but unfortunately thieves are reluctant to keep records. We can mention also, for example, the conclusion made following an inspection at that time in the Ministry of Municipal Services (kommunal'nogo khoziaistva) of the Ukraine that 40 percent of all appliances, parts, and materials used for repairs were stolen annually. Again, it is difficult to judge if the estimate was accurate, though no one is interested in exaggerating a bad situation. Certainly the problem is very serious. Many social considerations are involved, but we are examining the situation only from an economic standpoint.

Although managers may participate in this kind of stealing, it is characteristic primarily of the lower levels in the hierarchy. Managerial theft is less explicit, and even legal. It involves the violation of the rules of the game of planning or "financial discipline." As mentioned above, such violations are inevitable if managers want to fulfill their responsibilities. But this can be classified as stealing from the society's point of view if it is done for personal gain. Let us consider an example.

A shoe factory manufactures boots which are allocated to a trade organization. The latter cannot sell the boots because of their poor quality, and keeps them on the shelves of its stores for years. Eventually they are thrown away or sold for almost nothing. However the director and other managers of the factory are interested in manufacturing as many boots as possible since the transfer of boots to the trade organization is a sale for them. If there were not constraints on wage funds, they would continue to exceed the plan targets for boots, receiving additional raw materials from their suppliers by any means, including bribes, and paying their employees extra bonuses. In many situations it is more important for planning authorities to limit wages than to plan additional output without such limits.

Here the question may arise as to why the above sales should be nominal rather than real. The standard answer is that the system of material supply would be responsible for such a develoment. As we discussed earlier, this system is by no means effective. But what would happen if it were eliminated? The enterprises and organizations would not become more responsible for the inputs they utilize. Nor would they stop selling the "boots" to each other. On the contrary, an appropriate choice of contracts could benefit all involved (except of course the consumer). Since the elimination of the system of material supply would not automatically increase the availability of commodities, for the trade organization poor boots will still be better than nothing. Indeed all the incentive provisions of the 1965 Reform proved these arguments. Fulfillment of plan targets, resulting in the growth of wages and bonuses, grew considerably in the first years of the Reform without much real effect on the quantity and quality of output.

Despite organizational changes, inputs will still be free for enterprises and organizations. Without competition among products, it will not be possible to judge whether manufactured products are in real demand in the economy and whether the incentive funds flow in the right direction. We could continue along these lines, but do not want to depart too greatly from reality. We will emphasize only that the incentive provisions of the 1965 Reform came into conflict with the principle of separation of economic decision making from possible gains.

All of this shows that the "separation principle" is important for a Soviet-type economy and therefore makes the concept of decentralization specific for this economy. It cannot be viewed straightforwardly in terms of the enterprises versus bureaucracy. Since enterprises are separated from the real process of decision making, the structure of the decision-making level characterizes the degree of the centralization of the economy. If decision making is concentrated in one center, the economy tends toward centralization. If it is distributed among many such centers, the economy may tend, ceteris paribus, toward decentralization.

From this standpoint, the national economic councils (sovnarkhozy) of Krushchev's period, with decision-making powers dispersed among many territorial centers, represented a move toward some decentralization. They were more flexible in applying the command principle to the economy than the previous and subsequent branch structure of management. The branch structure reestablished by the 1965 Reform was indeed a tendency toward centralization of the economy since it concentrated the decision-making process in one center. Therefore the 1965 Reform with its restructuring of the economy and incentive provisions was self-contradictory. Only its first group of measures, restructuring of the economy, conformed to the principle of separation of decisions and gains, and these received further development in the 1970s. Almost all decisions related to the second group, incentive provisions, were gradually abandoned.

This explanation is important for understanding future developments in the Soviet economy. If we cannot expect radical changes in regard to the economic

responsibility of industrial enterprises, it is senseless to talk about extending more economic prerogatives
to them. As discussed above, the system of incentives
directs all economic units toward participation in
profits, while the economy needs participation in
losses. The only known principle of collective economic responsibility for enterprise operations is the
sharing of equity ownership with participation both in
profits and losses. It would however be unrealistic to
try to develop any model of collective equity ownership
for Soviet enterprises since the problem of property
ownership is too complex for such a simple approach.
What remains is to think in terms of the distribution
of decision making among the levels of managerial
hierarchy.

We do not declare this a solution to the problem of
centralization and decentralization of the economy.
Unfortunately we do not think a solution exists at all.
The decentralization of the decision-making process is
merely a possible rational development under existing
political and economic conditions. Horizontal structures, similar to sovnarkohy for example, are a likely
model for such a development. Important in this
respect is that the structure of the decision-making
process in the party hierarchy changes in the same
direction, i.e., in favor of local party authorities.

THE SLOWDOWN IN ECONOMIC GROWTH:  WHO IS RESPONSIBLE?

The slowdown in Soviet economic growth has become a
popular topic for discussion. Analysts the world over
seek to discover whether the phenomenon is temporary or
permanent. Although the theme appears beyond the scope
of our study, some of its aspects are indeed related.
Of greater importance is uncovering the reasons behind
such a slowdown which could be helpful in examining the

economy's prospects for the future. The table below, which contains official Soviet data, follows the growth of a few important indicators and shows targets for the present plan [14].*

TABLE 5.1
Growth of Main Macroindicators (%)

| Indicator | 1966-70 | 1971-75 | 1976-80 | 1981-85 (plan) |
|---|---|---|---|---|
| National Income | 41 | 28 | 21 | 18 |
| Gross Value of Industrial Output | 50 | 43 | 24 | 26 |
| Gross Value of Agricultural Output (avg. annual data) | 21 | 13 | 9 | 13 |
| Fixed Capital Investment | 43 | 42 | 29 | 11 |
| Labor Productivity | 39 | 25 | 17 | 20 |

The data show the scale of the general decline in economic growth in the observed fifteen-year period. They are especially interesting since the targets for the 11th Five-Year Plan are very modest, and we know that five-year plans traditionally are not met. However the scale of the slowdown and its consequences are not the subject of our study. Nor are we going to explain why steady economic growth is much more important for the Soviet economy than for free-market economies. What we will do is analyze briefly the main factors that are in our opinion responsible for the slowdown, and then proceed to a discussion of prospects for the future.

We do not claim of course to present all the fac-

*See the footnote on page 104.

tors responsible, if this is possible. Our aim is to explain the slowdown in economic growth from the standpoint of problems noted in the discussion of the evolution of the planning system. We will proceed on a purely economic basis, ignoring the numerous social problems that also play a part. The following simple relationship is implied:

$$r_Q = r_\ell \cdot R_L + r_L,$$

where $r_Q$ = the rate of increase in output Q in current period t, i.e., $r_Q = \dfrac{Q_t}{Q_{t-1}} - 1$;

$R_L$ = the growth ratio of manpower L in current period t, i.e., $R_L = \dfrac{L_t}{L_{t-1}}$ ;

$r_L$ = the rate of increase in manpower L in current period t, i.e., $r_L = R_L - 1$;

$r_\ell$ = the rate of increase in labor productivity $\ell$ $(\ell_t = \dfrac{Q_t}{L_t})$ in current period t, i.e., $r_\ell = \dfrac{\ell_t}{\ell_{t-1}} - 1$.

The above formula is an identity and therefore is always true. It relates the growth in output, labor productivity, and employment and shows that the rate of increase in output is the sum of two terms: the rate of increase in manpower and the rate of increase in labor productivity corrected by the growth ratio of manpower. Concerning the two factors affecting the growth of output, only employment is a primary one. Labor productivity depends on output and employment, and the latter is important not only because it is in the productivity denominator: the output in the numerator is not an independent factor since it varies with the change in employment according to the above formula.

If employment does not grow, the growth rate of

output is determined by the growth of productivity
only. Therefore in industries with decreasing
employment, in which technological change is not very
impressive, the decline in the growth of employment
results in a corresponding decline in the growth of
output. This is exactly what happened in the 10th
five-year period (1976-1980) in such industries as
coal, ferrous metallurgy, construction materials, and
woodworking. The output of coal, ferrous ores, steel,
rolled metal, cement, and cellulose remained at levels
attained at the end of the previous five-year period.
Of course other factors besides manpower do affect
these industries. For example, extracting ores and
coal in overworked basins becomes more and more difficult. In the coal industry there is even a special
fund provided to keep up output levels.

It is probably too early to consider the depletion
of reserves as a factor in the slowdown of the above
industries. It is evidently not a factor in the
construction materials and woodworking industries.
Concerning metallurgy, the Soviet Union has sufficient
ferrous ores, even in its European sector. Nor are the
future prospects considered bad for coal and natural
gas. Indeed the Soviets intend to place a new emphasis
on coal and gas development after taking into account
the worsening petroleum situation. Table 5.2 provides
present and future production figures.*

The planned growth in coal and gas production is
possible only with increased expenditures on labor.
Such expenditures are particularly important because of
the decline in the number of highly productive fuel
deposits in the total number explored [36]. Conse-
sequently extraction consumes everincreasing amounts of

*See the footnote on page 104.

TABLE 5.2
The Increase of Output of Fuels in Absolute Values

| Fuel | 1976-80 | 1981-85 (plan) |
|------|---------|----------------|
| Petroleum, million metric t | 112 | 27 |
| Gas, billion sq. m | 146 | 195 |
| Coal, million metric t | 15 | 59 |

labor and capital. Since investment is planned at the level of capacities of the construction industry and industries producing capital goods, it is influenced by labor considerations too. In discussions of the Soviet economy, the shortage of manpower is one of the major topics, along with, for example, petroleum production and the role of weather in agriculture. Table 5.3 illustrates employment in industry (promyshlenno-proizvodstvennyi personal) based on 1965-1979 data [32].

Although the slowdown in industrial employment growth has stabilized in the last two five-year periods at a level of eight percent, the absolute yearly increases in the 10th five-year period form a sharply diminishing pattern. For 1981-1985 Soviet sources see industrial employment growth at a rate of no more than three percent [25]. Thus economic growth will be determined completely by the growth of labor productivity and will be almost equal to it according to the above formula. On the other hand, the Soviet economy depends highly on extensive factors of growth which will be restrained by scarce manpower. Having explained the role of manpower in limiting extensive growth, we will now return to the problems of productivity and labor shortages noted in Chapter 2. The

TABLE 5.3
Industrial Employment and Its Growth

| Indicator | 1965 | 1970 | 1975 | 1976 | 1977 | 1978 | 1979 | 1980 (est.) |
|---|---|---|---|---|---|---|---|---|
| Employment, thousands of men | 27,447 | 31,593 | 34,054 | 34,815 | 35,417 | 36,014 | 36,446 | 36,850 |
| Increase over five years, % | | 15 | 8 | | | | | 8 |
| Absolute increase during a year, thousands of men | | 829 (avg) | 492 (avg) | 761 | 602 | 597 | 432 | 404 |

concept of demand for labor cannot be defined for the Soviet economy in the same manner as for a free-market economy. Even if certain products manufactured by the Soviet economy are in demand, one cannot be certain that a derived demand for labor is justified: this depends on labor and wage policies and the effect on them of political and social considerations. If changes in these policies result in a change in the demand for manpower while other plan targets are equal, we can suspect that the level of demand is set artificially.

Many experiments, including the Shchekino experiment mentioned above, proved that under certain circumstances the number employed could be reduced dramatically. These experiments were conducted on a very limited scale and kept under strict control by the supervising ministries and local and central party authorities. The experiments were terminated in the 1970s and, as wage policies became more rigid, enterprises became increasingly reluctant to lay off workers. If they did so, they would be seen as refusing to accept intensive plans, with raised plan targets as a consequence.

A corollary to the above considerations is that the Soviet economy has the potential for decreasing the size of the work force without a decline in the level of output. The result would be a growth in productivity and in reserves of manpower. However this potential will not necessarily be exploited or even discovered. Indeed its existence matters little at present since the real problem lies in the nature of the system itself. We might point out that the country is not ready for large-scale layoffs, and the political and social implications of such actions are well known. Further, there does exist a sort of equilibrium of income among different social groups that would be distorted in such an event. Finally, if due to a growth in productivity more wages were spent in producing more goods, it would be necessary to have some evidence that the goods were in demand. Otherwise, with commodities allocated through the system of material supply, output could grow, as explained above, without real impact on sales to consumers. This would mean that limitations on wages were more valuable than increases in output. Although all these problems form a closed circle, the mere fact of the existence of the potential for productivity growth without technological change may be of great importance in the future.

In the above formula the rate of increase in output depends on other factors which affect productivity as well as manpower. Technological change is of course the main factor in this case. In our econometric research we tried to estimate the impact on output and productivity of technological change measured either as endogenous or exogenous with respect to a given model. Only in machine-building data, a pronounced effect of factors that could be associated with technological change, not with the growth of inputs, was observed. Yet even here one could not eliminate the role of increasing prices since goods of improved quality (tovary s uluchshennymi tekhniko-ekonomicheskimi svoistvami) are considered completely new. Put differently, when the growth of prices is hidden by the introduction of new products, it is impossible to eliminate their influence on the growth of that part of output which is explained by technological change.

The availability and quality of raw materials is another important factor influencing output and productivity. While we noted this problem for the areas of fuel, energy, and metal, nothing has been said about industries turning out consumer goods. Their dependence on raw materials is fixed in planning technology:

the sequence of calculations for light industry and the food industry begins with the determination of inputs allocated to these industries. As the main supplier to light and food industries, agriculture affects the national product directly and through these industries. Together with them, agriculture accounts for about half the national income. Poor performance in agriculture restrains the growth of half the economy and affects the whole economy by lowering the standards of living. Our comments on agriculture will hardly be new but are worth repeating here.

It is common to blame the failures of Soviet agriculture on the weather. When I first heard such talk from planning authorities at the beginning of the 1970s, I was surprised: it had always been held that there could be no obstacles to the meeting of high goals, and planning authorities could not violate this principle on their own. But we must note that in the 1951-1965 fifteen-year period agriculture output declined only twice (1951, 1963), while in the 1966-1980 period it was down six times (1969, 1972, 1974, 1975, 1979, and 1980). Evidently the propagandists decided that it was better to blame the weather for the failures than something else. However we do not believe that we have to accept without question the assertion that in 1966-1980 the weather was three times worse than in 1951-1965.

One may argue that, all else being equal, the better the weather the greater the harvest. For Soviet agriculture today, "good" weather means no deviation from ideal weather conditions during all of the year's seasons. The probability of such ideal weather is low, and an American farmer would certainly not have the same thought in mind when speaking of good weather.

The poor agricultural records of the Soviet kolkhozy and sovkhozy are well known, but there are

always new developments some of which are of interest.
Unintentionally Krushchev began a long-term trend of
deterioration in the country's food supply when he
introduced a system of wage payments in kolkhozy.
Krushchev wanted to end Stalin's agricultural policy of
robbing the peasant population. Indeed he did bring a
dramatic improvement in the peasants' standard of
living and increased to some extent their incentive to
work on kolkhoz fields. On the other hand, he
destroyed their willingness to raise produce on private
plots and sell it to state purchasing organizations.
Until then the peasants had been allowed to buy goods
from the stores of the state purchasing organizations
only in exchange for their products. The positive
impact of the new policy proved only temporary, since
the cash incentives meant little to the peasants if
they could not buy building materials, motorcycles,
cars, etc.

The negative effect of a noncompensated reduction
in the output of private plots. (priusadebnye uchastki)
is what the economy is forced to endure. While the
output of the public sector of agriculture reportedly
grew by 18 percent in 1979 relative to 1970, in the
private sector it shrank by one percent [32]. We
usually accept such information with reservations.
First, since according to doctrine the role of the private sector must by definition decrease, the truth may
be altered. Second, figures on output in the private
sector, prices in kolkhoz markets, etc., are obtained
in planning by estimate rather than direct calculation,
and so are very unreliable. Nonetheless there are
other indicators that support the conclusion that the
private sector in agriculture has declined.

Doubtless the nation could not survive without such
a sector. According to official sources, which must be
considered with the above reservations, in 1979 the

private sector produced 59 percent of the potatoes, 31 percent of the other vegetables, 30 percent of the meat, 29 percent of the milk, and 33 percent of the eggs [32] on only about one percent of the total agricultural land. One should also note that the productivity of Soviet peasants is usually held to be lower than that of farmers in the West due to a lack of skills, technology, and other advantages [2]. In view of this, the productivity and skills of these people, mostly women, seem to work miracles. Farming the worst pieces of land after the main work at the kolkhoz has been finished and toiling without benefit of machines or fertilizers, these peasants manage to feed with the above products nearly a third of the nation.

Soviet leaders have always been sensitive to the existence of the private sector in agriculture. Besides ideological and social considerations, the private sector pointed up the leaders' inability to improve the public sector despite numerous resolutions of the Central Committee, enormous investment in agriculture, and forced labor contributed by students, army troops, and urban dwellers. The leaders would probably attempt to abolish this sector once and for all if it did not play such a vital role in keeping the peasants on the kolkhozy: if no one in a peasant family works in a kolkhoz, the family cannot have a private plot.

There is a new development in this area that could be important for the future. The continued sovkhoz and kolkhoz failures have forced the leadership to turn attention to the private sector once again. During 1977-1980 the Central Committee adopted several resolutions encouraging the development of private agriculture not only by peasants but by urban dwellers too. Small plots of land (dachi) near forests, lakes, and rivers are very popular with urban dwellers. However it is difficult for the average person to get one of these plots: one needs either special privileges or the money to secure such a plot from a person who has one for his use (the land is not private property).

The 1977 Resolution of the Central Committee and the Council of Ministers made it less difficult to get such plots and eased the restrictions on market gardening [42]. Enterprises can receive land for their employees from the State Reserve (Gosudarstvennyi zapas) and from surplus kolkhoz and sovkhoz lands. Those who have plots may also raise various domestic animals including cows -- which was prohibited before -- and improve the land by building small houses. Enterprises may spend up to 25 percent of the social fund (fond sotsial'nogo razvitiia i zhilishchnogo stroitel'stva) on lands received by their employees for private use. In rural areas sovkhozy and other state organizations must help peasants to provide feed for their cattle and to plow their lands. Finally, those who sell products to state purchasing organizations have priorioty in buying goods which are in short supply.

Another development in this area is the creation of agricultural subsidiaries at industrial enterprises. Forced by the haphazard requests of local party organizations to send employees to work on agricultural projects, enterprises began to request permission to have their own permanent agricultural concerns. This would give them the possibility to coordinate agricultural work with production operations, not to mention buying cheap food for their cafeterias. Some ministries such as those for coal, petroleum, and nonferrous metallurgy organized the subsidiaries themselves, but other ministries were reluctant to do so. As it turned out, however, organizing these subsidiaries did not free enterprises from sending large teams of employees to kolkhozy and sovkhozy to "help" with agricultural work.

In 1978 the Central Committee and the Council of Ministers adopted a resolution forcing all the ministries to create agricultural subsidiaries at their enterprises [43]. Beginning in 1980, Gosplan had to allocate tractors, combines, fertilizers, and other inputs to the agricultural subsidiaries of industrial enterprises. Enterprises were also allowed to hire additional employees for agricultural work according to limits and norms determined by supervising ministries.

These developments introduced some new tendencies in recent agricultural policy even though they are not new in principle. It is too early to judge their direct effects. Much depends on whether they will merely retain an appearance of activity or turn into a long-term strategy. Evidently the present leadership is not interested in creating complications for itself by running risky long-term experiments. But for their successors, the trend may be an attractive way of solving the kolkhoz dilemma.

SOME SPECULATIONS ON PROSPECTS

In analyzing tendencies in the development of the Soviet planning system, we tried to point out factors that might provide insights into the future. This takes on greater importance as Soviet leaders grow older. The easiest approach to the Soviet economy would be to say that everything is wrong and must be changed. But such assertions usually stop at that since the mechanisms for such overall changes are unknown. Moreover, while large-scale transformations may be attractive in theory, their implementation can be disastrous. Another complication stems from the fact that economic alterations are subject to political principles and personal changes in leadership. We hope that an evolutionary change of leadership will take place. Only someone with the worst motivations would desire radical change with its possible bloody consequences. In any case, in discussing expectations we will consider the possible development of events rather than ideas for what should be done in the economy. By development of events we mean only a tendency, i.e., something that is true on the average and by direction.

Recent Soviet history demonstrates that, in an effort to gain control over the bureaucratic apparatus created by predecessors, new Soviet leaders begin their terms with economic reforms. In keeping with these objectives, the most critical aim of the last two reforms -- in 1957 and 1964 -- was organizational. Along with major organizational changes, the problem of inefficiency was examined. In each case provisions were made to consider efficiency strictly within new organizational structures.

What direction will an economic reform initiated by new leaders take? The foundations of the planned economy restrict the range for organizational restructuring. Only two principles of organization -- the vertical branch and territorial principles -- have been employed. Mixed structures are possible only in the sense that some industries are organized on the vertical principle and others on the horizontal. But a single industry cannot use both at one time. This is a consequence of the "addressing character" (adresnyi kharakter) of the plan according to which resources for enterprises are to be allocated to their supervising organizations which are the resource holders (fondoderzhateli). This eliminates the possibility of double supervision of industries and their enterprises. Based on these considerations, we can expect a new economic reform to be directed toward horizontal, i.e., territorial organizations.

Evidently, for reasons of prestige, such a reform cannot be a complete replica of past models. Khrushchev's national economic councils were based on the provincial administrative units (oblasti) of large republics. Of course many other divisions are possible, for instance based on the major economic regions of the country. There are ten such regions in the RSFSR -- Northwest, Central, Volga-Vyatka, Black Earth Central, Volga, North Caucasus, Ural, West Siberia, East Siberia, and Far East -- and three in the Ukraine -- Donetsk-Dnepr, Southwest, and South. Other economic regions include the Baltic, Transcaucasus, Central Asia, Kazakhstan, Belorussia, and Moldavia.

In recent years discussion has taken place, at least at the level of methodological and organizational problems, on territorial industrial complexes (territorial'no-promyshlennye kompleksy) and agrarian industrial complexes (agrarno-promyshlennye kompleksy). These are groups of industries in an economic region of the country related to a dominant industry which determines, to some extent, the final results of their operations.

Criticizing Khrushchev's structure of national economic councils, economists emphasized that these were unable to pursue the unique branch technical policy which is the only way to technological change. Nonetheless, shortly after the 1965 Reform discussion began on the coordination of the branch and territorial principles of management and planning. One reason was that a duality had been created by the vertical administrative hierarchy and horizontal party subordination of enterprises, if we take into account that the latter assumes administrative supervision as well. Further, the branch principle of planning fails to take into consideration interindustrial dependence on local sources of labor, water supply, opportunity cost of

lands, sewage systems, transportation, road construction, pollution problems, etc. Last, local authorities
became dissatisfied with their minor role in decision
making in industries of union and union-republic subordination. As is typical in propagandistic exercises,
the same "unique branch technical policy" has gradually
been turned against the branch principle: industrial
operations are isolated from each other, and their
technological decisions are not coordinated.

The above-mentioned territorial industrial complexes became fashionable as a solution to the problem
of coordinating branch and territorial principles of
management. Large-scale projects for extracting petroleum and gas in Siberia required coordination of the
operations of different ministries. Because of their
common goals, the projects were declared to be the
developments of the territorial industrial complexes.
The largest of these are the West Siberia Petroleum and
Gas Complex and the Kansk-Achinsk Fuel and Energy
Complex. Several other chemical complexes such as the
Tobol'sk, Tomsk, and Achinsk are planned. In addition,
plans for the development of various machine-building
complexes have been suggested. These examples
illustrate the confusion resulting from the dominant
role of the branch principle of management in the
classification of complexes. If the territorial principle were followed, the West Siberia Complex, for
example, would include, along with petroleum and gas
industries, chemical production, machine building for
the industries involved, and construction, transportation, and consumer good industries.

At present there is no specific planning or management at the interindustrial level within territorial
complexes. As is customary, Gosplan attends to these
questions in the process of planning and allocating
resources. The only difference is that more funds for

housing and social measures are allocated directly to the ministries whose industries are associated with the complex than would be otherwise. Such complexes may play an important role in the future restructuring of the economy, especially when the specialization of an economic region is pronounced. In this respect, even the manufacture of military hardware would not create problems because, with few exceptions, all economic regions are specialized in this field.

Would the territorial principle of management be more efficient than the existing branch principle? The history of organizational changes demonstrates that they did not bring much improvement. On the other hand, a system based on a complete lack of economic responsibility provides almost no flexibility. Its possibilities for decentralizing the economy are limited to redistributing decision making among the various levels of supervision and control of enterprises and organizations. We formulated above the principle of separating decision making from possible gains, which helps to protect against lack of economic responsibility. According to this definition, the territorial principle is a move toward a certain amount of decentralization since it means the division of decision making among several levels of management. Thus its implementation would mean redistribution of decision making in favor of local authorities. Therefore the territorial principle may be the lesser of two evils.

Along with organizational restructuring of the economy, new leaders will have to demonstrate their willingness and ability to solve serious problems. Among them is the growth of productivity and manpower. Usually analysts conclude that a lack of advanced technology is responsible for the low level of Soviet productivity. This is a standard explanation in terms of

production functions, but these can be used for international comparisons only if other conditions are
equal. Certainly that is not the case here. Besides
the state of technology and levels of capital and manpower used, productivity in Soviet industry is a function of the policy of planning the size of the work
force, wages, and wage rate control.

The paradox in the planning of manpower was
explained above. On the one hand, the economy needs a
larger work force in eastern regions and in specific
industries. Therefore the limit on employees is one of
the main planning indicators designated by the 1979
Resolution. (In the 1965 Resolution it had been considered only as a reference for substantiating wage
fund demands.) On the other hand, the policy of
planning and wage rate control contributed to
unwillingness on the part of enterprises to reduce the
size of their work force. With such reductions they
would make their plan targets tougher without the
possibility of increasing wages for the remaining
employees. Moreover, from the beginning of the 1965
Reform party authorities at all levels opposed large-
scale layoffs of workers.

What we tried to make clear in this respect is that
the Soviet economy possesses potentials for productivity growth which have nothing to do with the state
of technology. An analyst familiar with recent Soviet
employment policies will find many indicators of
overstated demands for labor. Numerous experiments,
like the Shchekino one discussed above, proved that
under special provisions for wage rate growth enterprises were able to meet their plan targets with significantly reduced numbers of workers.

The normative approach to planning wages and incentive funds introduced by the 1979 Resolution can have
some impact in the future too. Despite strict control,

the possibility for wage funds to increase in relation to the growth of output will probably result in the increase of average wage rates. This in turn will augment the demand for scarce raw materials and their role as a deterrent to the growth of productivity.

These and other aspects of the problem of productivity and manpower illustrate the difficulties new leaders will face. Unlike organizational changes, this problem cannot be separated from others at the heart of the economy. New leaders will be able to reduce employment levels at existing enterprises and keep the output unchanged only with substantial raises in wage rates. But if manufactured goods are distributed through the system of material supply, it will remain unknown whether they are in real demand and therefore whether wage growth is justified. On the other hand, the supply system cannot be eliminated if enterprises do not share in economic responsibility. It is senseless to imitate even limited markets and competition when national resources belong to no one.

Most likely the new leaders will not undertake fundamental changes in the economic system, but will pursue a policy of reducing manpower at existing enterprises, continuing regulated "experiments" like the Shchekino one. The experiments of course will be very costly. Their regulation is another concern. Reductions in manpower are desirable in some industries but undesirable in others such as coal production, metallurgy, and construction. The national system for the redistribution of unassigned workers (the unemployed) among industries and regions must operate. One of the questions in this respect is how to influence someone to go to work in Siberia when he or she would prefer not to. The question was easy to answer in Stalin's time but not at present and, we would hope, not in the future. Soviet leaders have tried unsuccessfully to find its solution for the Central Asian republics where there is a large potential reserve work force. The low "social mobility" of the local population negates projections by the central planning authorities.

All of these points help to show that the Soviet economy possesses the potential for growth of productivity and, from that, economic growth in general. Everything will depend on how this potential can be realized in the future. From this standpoint, we can say that the present slowdown in Soviet economic growth is not necessarily permanent.

As stressed above, the involvement of unassigned manpower in the production process will not guarantee productivity growth. In other words, it is not always possible to make use of additional manpower. The reason is that the scarcity of raw materials, especially those supplied by agriculture, may become the decisive constraint. That new leaders will attempt to find a final solution to the agriculture problem is not new. The question is of course how they will do so within their political and ideological limits.

In our opinion, recent developments in agriculture can have some impact in the future as their scale is expanded. These developments are the growth of land in private use and the spread of agricultural subsidiaries of industrial enterprises. Their future consequences include a decline in the dependence of the population on the supply of foods by kolkhozy and sovkhozy: increased involvement of the urban population in agricultural work; gradual elimination of kolkhozy by distributing their lands for private use and transforming them into sovkhozy; and specialization of sovkhozy in the production of meat and commodities such as grain, cotton, sugar beets, etc., which are not grown on plots in private use.

The incomparably higher productivity of the private

agriculture sector is acknowledged by Soviet leaders. They accept also the fact that kolkhozy and sovkhozy are unable to supply the population with vegetables, milk, eggs, meat, etc. The logical step for new leaders would be to convert the privilege of using a piece of land in a rural area to common practice. Most workers are peasants by birth and, if land is distributed, will work willingly for themselves.

There are no official statistics on how much of the work force from urban areas is used in agriculture. From April through November thousands of people are sent each day to kolkhozy and sovkhozy. Having participated in this work for many years, I can say that its productivity is very low. Even while responsible for research projects, I spent an average of two weeks a year in manual labor (as compared with three months when I was in the lower social position of a student). Sometimes, however, when enterprises are able to create good working conditions and pay more than regular salaries, young people participate in agricultural work without outside pressure.

Finding it difficult to secure large teams for kolkhozy and sovkhozy, especially during weekends and on a weekly or monthly basis, administrators at enterprises and organizations have already begun to consider this component in hiring. From this standpoint, the most desirable candidates are single young people, and the least desirable are mothers with small children and the elderly. Some enterprises would find it beneficial to run their own farms. They could keep special teams for that purpose rather than sending their employees to kolkhozy at the request of local party authorities. Rural settlements are collapsing, and agricultural subsidiaries of industrial enterprises can become at least a weak remedy. While a solution to the problem would be to attract people to settle in villages and work in agriculture, such a large-scale program is beyond the powers of Soviet leaders in the foreseeable future.

The increase of land in private use and agricultural subsidiaries of industrial enterprises would increase the participation of urban dwellers in agricultural work. By the same token, it would make the urban population less dependent on kolkhozy, sovkhozy, and "weather." Highly specialized sovkhozy will probably replace kolkhozy in all areas. In the future they will have to use seasonal workers, hiring them at competitive wage rates.

None of the changes in the Soviet economy discussed here seem too encouraging in the long run. They do not address the fundamental weakness of the economic system as a whole. Not wishing to indulge in fantasy, we did not present long-term solutions based on the changes in the system. Our fragmentary speculations are founded on several assumptions. The main one is that the transition of political leadership will be accomplished smoothly and from the top. The next assumption, which is a corollary to the first, is that new leaders will preserve the fundamentals of the existing economic system. Given this and assuming that new leaders will be rational, we developed a fragmentary scenario of some possible alterations in organizational, methodological, and economic principles of planning and management.

# References

1. Abalkin, L. "Ekonomicheskaia strategiia partii i 11i piatiletnii plan" (The Economic Strategy of the Party and the 11th Five-Year Plan). Planovoe khoziaistvo, 3 (1981).
2. Abouchar, A. Economic Evaluation of Soviet Socialism. Elmsford, N.Y.: Pergamon Press (1979).
3. Anufrienko, S. "Khoziaistvennaia reforma i initsiativa predpriiatii" (The Economic Reform and the the Initiative of the Enterprise). Voprosy ekonomiki, 12 (1968).
4. Bachurin, A. "Povyshenie deistvennosti plana i khoziaistvennaia reforma" (Improving Plan Effectiveness and the Economic Reform). Planovoe khoziaistvo, 7 (1980).
5. Bandera, V. N. and Z. L. Melnyk (ed.). The Soviet Economy in Regional Perspective. N.Y.: Praeger (1973).
6. Berliner, J. The Innovation Decision in Soviet Industry. Cambridge: The MIT Press (1976).
7. Budavei, V., et al. "Metodicheskie osnovy postroeniia ASPR" (The Concepts of the Automated System of Planning Calculations). Planovoe khoziaistvo, 11 (1974).
8. Chistiakov, M. "Novye Metodicheskie ukazaniia k razrabotke gosudarstvennykh planov" (The New Methodological Directions for the Development of National Economic Plans). Planovoe khoziaistvo, 7 (1980).
9. Drogichinskii, N. "Voprosy razrabotki general'nykh skhem upravleniia otraslevymi sistemami" (The Outline of Branch Organizational Structures). Planovoe khoziaistvo, 3 (1973).
10. Emel'ianov, A. S. and F. I. Kushnirsky. Modelirovanie pokazatelei razvitiia ekonomiki soiuznoi respubliki (Modeling Economic Growth in the Republic). Moscow: Ekonomika (1974).

11. Fedorenko, N. P. O razrabotke sistemy optimal'nogo funktsionirovaniia ekonomiki (The Foundations of the Optimally Functioning Economy). Moscow: Nauka (1968).
12. Gorshkov, M. "O stoimostnoi otsenke ob'ema promyshlennoi produktsii" (The Value Estimation of Industrial Output). Planovoe khoziaistvo, 8 (1980).
13. Isaev, V. "Nekotorye voprosy khoziaistvennoi reformy v stroitel'stve" (Some Problems of the Economic Reform in Construction). Voprosy ekonomiki, 5 (1970).
14. Ivanov, E. and A. Balashova. "Tempy i proportsii 11i piatiletki" (Growth and Proportions in the 11th Five-Year Plan). Planovoe khoziaistvo, 4 (1981).
15. Jun', O. "Napravleniia sovershenstvovaniia planirovaniia pri sozdanii vtoroi ocheredi ASPR" (The Second Stage of the Development of the Automated System of Planning Calculations). Planovoe khoziaistvo, 10 (1978).
16. Kalinin, I. "Sovershenstvovanie sistemy material'-nykh balansov i normativnoi bazy planirovaniia" (Improvements in the System of Material Balances and the Normative Base of Planning). Planovoe khoziaistvo, 8 (1980).
17. Katsenelinboigen, A. Studies in Soviet Economic Planning. White Plains, N.Y.: Sharpe (1978).
18. Kirichenko, V., et al. "Tsentral'nyi kompleks planovykh raschetov -- vedushchee zveno vtoroi ocheredi ASPR" (The Central Complex Subsystem in the Automated System of Planning Calculations). Planovoe khoziaistvo, 10 (1980).
19. Klotsvog, F. "Ispol'zovanie mezhotraslevogo balansa v praktike planirovaniia" (The Application of Input-Output Tables in Planning). Planovoe khoziaistvo, 1 (1980).
20. Koropeckyi, I. S. and G. E. Schroeder (ed.). Economics of Soviet Regions. N.Y.: Praeger (1981).
21. Krylov, P. "Godovye plany v sisteme piatiletnego planirovaniia" (The Annual Targets in Five-Year Planning). Planovoe khoziaistvo, 6 (1980).
22. Lebedinskii, N. "Razvitie narodnokhoziaistvennogo planirovaniia i ASPR" (National Economic Planning and the Automated System of Planning Calculations). Planovoe khoziaistvo, 11 (1979).
23. Levine, H. S. "The Centralized Planning of Supply in Soviet Industry." In Comparisons of the U.S. and Soviet Union Economies. Washington: Joint Economic Committee (1959).
24. Liberman, E. G. Economic Methods and the Effectiveness of Production. N.Y.: International Arts

167

and Scientific Press (1971).
25. Literaturnaia Gazeta, 26 November 1980, p. 11.
26. Marx, K. Capital: A Critique of Political Economy.
    N.Y.: International Publishers (1967).
27. Masol, V. "Aktual'nye voprosy sochetaniia otras-
    levogo i territorial'nogo planirovaniia" (The
    Urgent Problems in Coordinating Branch and Terri-
    torial Planning). Planovoe khoziaistvo, 3 (1980).
28. Metodicheskie ukazaniia k sostavleniiu gosudar-
    stvennogo plana razvitiia narodnogo khoziaistva
    SSSR (The Methodological Directions for the
    Development of National Economic Plans). Moscow:
    Economika (1969).
29. "Metodicheskie ukazaniia o poriadke opredeleniia
    napriazhennosti planov" (The Methodological
    Instructions for Evaluating Intensive Plans).
    Planovoe khoziaistvo, 3 (1980).
30. "Metodicheskie ukazaniia o poriadke razrobotki i
    primenenia v planirovanii pokazatelia chistoi
    produktsii (normativnoi)" (The Methodological
    Instructions for Computing the Normative Net
    Value of Output). Planovoe khoziaistvo, 11
    (1979).
31. Moskalenko, V. "Novoe v planirovanii zarabotnoi
    platy" (New Trends in Wage Planning). Planovoe
    khoziaistvo, 1 (1980).
32. Narodnoe khoziaistvo SSSR v 1979 (Statistical Hand-
    book on the Soviet Economy). Moscow (1980).
33. Osadchenko, S. "Povyshenie roli khoziaistvennogo
    rascheta i ekonomicheskikh stimulov" (On the
    Improvement of Cost-Accounting and Economic
    Incentives). Planovoe khoziaistvo, 11 (1980).
34. Pasukanis (ed.). Piatnadtsat' let sovetskogo
    stroitel'stva, 1917-1932 (Fifteen Years of Soviet
    Political Construction). Moscow (1932).
35. Pokaraev, G. and A. Zaitsev. "Voprosy sovershen-
    stvovaniia normirovaniia material'nykh resursov"
    (Problems in Setting Material Expenditure Norms).
    Planovoe khoziaistvo, 8 (1979).
36. Popov, V. "Mineral'no-syr'evye resursy strany, ikh
    ispol'zovanie" (The Mineral Resources of the USSR
    and Their Utilization). Planovoe khoziaistvo, 4
    (1981).
37. Postanovlenie TsK KPSS i SM SSSR ot 30 sentiabria
    1965, Ob uluchshenii upravleniia promyshlennost'-
    iu (Resolution of the Central Committee of the
    CPSU and the USSR Council of Ministers of Sep.
    30, 1965 on Restructuring Industry Management).
    Resheniia partii i pravitel'stva po khoziaistven-
    nym voprosam (Decisions of the Party and Govern-
    ment on Economic Questions). Moscow: Politizdat,
    5 (1968).
38. Postanovlenie TsK KPSS i SM SSSR ot 4 oktiabria

168

1965, O sovershenstvovanii planirovaniia i usilenii ekonomicheskogo stimulirovaniia promysh- lennogo proizvodstva (Resolution of the Central Committee of the CPSU and the USSR Council of Ministers of Oct. 4, 1965 on Improving Planning and the Economic Stimulation of Industry). Resheniia partii i pravitel'stva po khoziaistvennym voprosam (Decisions of the Party and Government on Economic Questions). Moscow: Politizdat, 5 (1968).

39. Postanovlenie SM SSSR ot 15 avgusta 1966, O merakh po vnedreniiu v narodnoe khoziaistvo sistem setevogo planirovaniia i upravleniia na osnove setevykh grafikov (Resolution of the USSR Council of Ministers of Aug. 15, 1966 on the Introduction of Network Modeling in Planning and Management). Resheniia partii i pravitel'stva po khoziaistven- nym voprosam (Decisions of the Party and Govern- ment on Economic Questions). Moscow: Politizdat, 6 (1968).

40. Postanovlenie TsK KPSS ot 22 fevralia 1973, O ser'- eznykh nedostatkakh v organizatsii sluzhebnykh komandirovok i izlishestvakh v raskhodovanie sredstv na eti tseli (Resolution of the Central Committee of the CPSU of Feb. 22, 1973 on Misuses in the Organization of Business Trips). Reshe- niia partii i pravitel'stva po khoziaistvennym voprosam (Decisions of the Party and Government on Economic Questions). Moscow: Politizdat, 9 (1974).

41. Postanovlenie TsK KPSS i SM SSSR ot 2 marta 1973, O nekotorykh meropriiatiiakh po dal'neishemu sovershenstvovaniiu upravleniia promyshlennost'iu (Resolution of the Central Committee of the CPSU and the USSR Council of Ministers of Mar. 2, 1973 on Measures for the Reorganization of the Middle Level of Management. Resheniia partii i pravitel'stva po khoziaistvennym voprosam (Decisions of the Party and Government on Eco- nomic Questions). Moscow: Politizdat, 9 (1974).

42. Postanovlenie TsK KPSS i SM SSSR ot 14 sentiabria 1977, O lichnykh podsobnykh khoziaistvakh kol- khoznikov, rabochikh, sluzhashchikh i drugikh grazhdan i kollektivnom sadovodstve i ogorod- nichestve (Resolution of the Central Committee of the CPSU and the USSR Council of Ministers of Sep. 14, 1977 on the Private Use of Land and Cooperative Gardening and Farming). Resheniia partii i pravitel'stva po khoziaistvennym voprosam (Decisions of the Party and Government on Economic Questions). Moscow: Politizdat, 12 (1979).

43. Postanovlenie TsK KPSS i SM SSSR ot 4 dekabria

169

1978, O podsobnykh sel'skikh khoziaistvakh
predpriiatii, organizatsii i uchrezhdenii
(Resolution of the Central Committee of the CPSU
and the USSR Council of Ministers of Dec. 4, 1978
on the Agriculture Subsidiaries of Industrial
Enterprises and Organizations). Resheniia partii
i pravitel'stva po khoziaistvennym voprosam
(Decisions of the Party and Government on Economic Questions). Moscow: Politizdat, 12 (1979).
44. Postanovlenie TsK KPSS i SM SSSR ot 12 iiulia 1979,
Ob uluchshenii planirovaniia i usilenii vozdei-
stviia khoziaistvennogo mekhanizma na povyshenie
effektivnosti proizvodstva i kachestva raboty
(Resolution of the Central Committee of the CPSU
and the USSR Council of Ministers of Jul. 12,
1979 on Improving Planning and the Economic
Mechanism). Planovoe khoziaistvo, 9 (1979).
45. Protserov, S. "Lichnaia material'naia otvetstven-
nost' rukovoditelei predpriiatii" (Personal
Material Responsibility of Managers). Planovoe
khoziaistvo, 5 (1974).
46. Rzheshevskii, V. "Povyshenie effektivnosti obrazovaniia pooshchritel'nykh fondov" (Improving the
Effectiveness of the Bonus Fund). Planovoe
khoziaistvo, 3 (1973).
47. Slepykh, V. "Shchekinskii eksperiment" (The
Shchekino Experiment). Planovoe khoziaistvo, 8
(1968).
48. Sorokin, G. "Intensivnye faktory ekonomicheskogo
rosta" (The Intensive Factors of Economic
Growth). Planovoe khoziaistvo, 4 (1981).
49. Tarasov, N. "Effektivnost' i kachestvo -- glavnye
napravleniia razvitiia legkoi promyshlennosti"
(Efficiency and Quality are the Main Directions
of the Growth of Light Industry). Planovoe
khoziaistvo, 3 (1976).
50. Treml, V. G. (ed.). Studies in Soviet Input-Output
Analysis. N.Y.: Praeger (1977).
51. Ukrainskii, D. "Planirovanie proizvodstva produktsii v natural'nom vyrazhenii" (Planning of Output in Physical Terms). Planovoe khoziaistvo, 10
(1980).
52. Urinson, Ia. "Povyshenie effektivnosti ispol'zova-
niia ekonomiko-matematicheskikh modelei v ASPR"
(Improving the Efficiency of Mathematical Models
in the Automated System of Planning Calculations). Planovoe khoziaistvo, 6 (1978).
53. Vorob'ev, V. "O primenenii mezhotraslevogo balansa
v praktike planirovaniia" (On the Use of Input-
Output Tables in Planning). Planovoe khoziaistvo,
7 (1973).

# Index

Supreme Soviet, 66, 136

Tarasov, 84
Technological change, 28,
   45, 95, 99, 145, 148-
   149, 156; policy, 50
Territorial industrial
   complexes, 120, 156, 157
Theft, 71, 128, 138-139
Trade organizations, 37;
   sales, 113
Turnover tax, 14, 26, 31
Two departments, 7; means
   of production, 7-8, 34;
   consumer goods, 7-8, 13,
   26, 37, 39, 41, 51, 79,
   83, 92, 97, 112-113,
   135, 149, 157

Ukrainian Gosplan, 66,
   75, 130; Dept. of Agriculture, 78; Dept. of
   Housing, 78; Dept. of
   Light Industry, 86;
   Dept. of Municipal Services, 78; Summary Dept.
   of the National Economic
   Plan, 85, 130; Ministry
   of the Coal Industry,
   75; Ministry of Municipal Services, 139
Unfinished goods, 12-13;
   construction, 90, 104
United States, 1, 118
USSR, 1, 41-42, 104-105.
   See also Soviet Union

Wages, 13, 27, 29, 36,
   40-42, 46, 51-52, 56,
   96, 110, 137, 140, 149,
   159-160; control of, 20,
   46, 140, 148-149; growth
   of, 36, 140; rates of,
   36-37, 40, 42, 46, 159-
   160
War Communism, 5
Weather, role of, 99, 146,
   150
Western analysts, 72, 85,
   112, 115, 127; corres-
   pondents, 80; economic
   literature, 72, 99;
   entrepreneur, 137;
   stereotypes, 3

Workers, 5, 18, 27, 37, 41,
   44, 46, 160, 162; lay-
   offs of, 36-37, 42, 160
World energy crisis, 17